Christmas at the Palace

Christmas at the Palace

50+ FESTIVE HOLIDAY RECIPES

CAROLYN ROBB

PHOTOGRAPHS BY JOHN KERNICK

weldon**owen**

CONTENTS

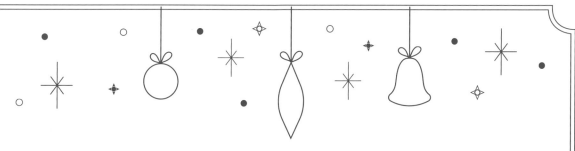

For Lucy, because no one loves the traditions, treats,
and tastes of Christmas more than you do.

INTRODUCTION

I ask you to answer me fairly: is not additional eating an ordinary Englishman's ordinary idea of Christmas Day?

—Anthony Trollope, *Orley Farm*, 1861–62

Today, just as in the Victorian era, Christmas Day is all about glorious food. Traditional British fare such as mince pies and figgy pudding with brandy butter, typically made according to treasured family recipes, are a must. The Christmas dinner of roast turkey with a bountiful array of accompaniments is an important part of the day, and many books offer directions for making the perfect gravy, sage-and-onion stuffing, and steamed Brussels sprouts. But scores of other fabulous Christmas Day treats are often overlooked.

This book is filled with inspiration, whimsy, a look back at the origins of some of our best-loved holiday traditions, and a wealth of Christmas cheer. Recipes for everything from pink sugar mice, ginger cakes, and spice-laced orange slices to smoked salmon parcels and bramble-infused vodka will appeal to cooks of all ages and abilities. Encompassing eight of Britain's most stunning fairy-tale palaces and castles, this collection sets the scene for a spectacular Christmas season of feasting with family and friends.

Happy Christmas and happy cooking!

Carolyn Robb

SANDRINGHAM HOUSE

Breakfast and Brunch

The excitement of a child waking up to find a bulging stocking from Father Christmas at the foot of the bed means that the day often starts well before the crack of dawn. By the time breakfast arrives, it feels more like lunchtime. Many families attend a morning church service. Others may embark on a Christmas morning walk for a breath of fresh air or to exercise their dogs (or children!). This chapter provides inspiration for an early breakfast or a leisurely midmorning brunch, an excellent precursor to the substantial traditional Christmas dinner served later in the day.

If you were fortunate enough to be celebrating Christmas at Sandringham House, the Norfolk County setting of the royal family's annual celebration, or even somewhere nearby, your breakfast or brunch could be almost entirely locally sourced. The Norfolk Black is considered the oldest turkey breed in the United Kingdom and could make the very finest turkey sandwich. The Sandringham estate farmers' market showcases an abundance of fabulous local foods produced both on and off the property, and one would surely be able to source blackberries to sit atop featherlight ricotta pancakes, freshly laid eggs for the perfect smoked salmon and scrambled egg parcels, or even some ancient grains to toss into a festive granola.

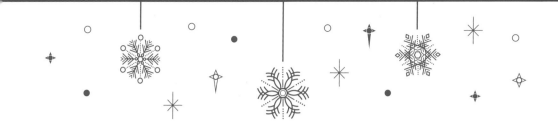

MINI CHOCOLATE AND CHERRY PANETTONE

Soaking the cherries and apricots in Madeira makes these little panettone into
something utterly irresistible—a worthy Christmas indulgence. Served warm,
alongside a big mug of coffee, they are the perfect start to the day.

⅔ cup (100 g) dried cherries

¾ cup (100 g) dried apricots, diced

⅓ cup (75 ml) Madeira

3¾ teaspoons active dry yeast

1 teaspoon superfine sugar

⅔ cup (160 ml) milk, warmed
(105°–115°F/40°–46°C)

4 cups (500 g) 00 flour (see
Chef's Note), plus more for
the work surface

1 teaspoon salt

¼ cup (50 g) firmly packed light
brown sugar

1 teaspoon pure vanilla extract

5 eggs, lightly beaten, plus a little
more for brushing

¾ cup plus 2 tablespoons (200 g)
butter, at room temperature

½ cup plus 1½ tablespoons (100 g)
small dark chocolate chips

Finely grated zest of 2 oranges

¼ cup (50 g) pearl sugar (see
Chef's Note) for finishing

Makes 12 small breads

In a bowl, combine the cherries, apricots, and Madeira and let stand
at room temperature for at least 1 hour but preferably for 24 hours.

In a small bowl, combine the yeast, superfine sugar, and warm milk
and let stand until frothy, about 10 minutes.

In a stand mixer fitted with the dough hook, combine the flour, salt,
brown sugar, vanilla, eggs, and yeast mixture and beat on low speed
for 2 minutes. Increase the speed to medium and mix until a soft
dough forms, 6–8 minutes. Gradually add the butter in small pieces
and mix for 6–8 minutes longer, stopping occasionally to scrape
down the bowl sides to ensure the dough is well mixed. The dough
will be very soft. Add the soaked fruit and any unabsorbed Madeira,
the chocolate chips, and the orange zest and mix until they are
evenly incorporated.

Tip the dough into a bowl, cover with plastic wrap, and chill the
dough until it has firmed up enough for it to be shaped, at least
8 hours or up to overnight.

Have ready 12 paper panettone or dariole molds', each about
2½ inches (6 cm) by 3 inches (7.5 cm), arranging them on a large
sheet pan, or line a 12-cup standard muffin pan with parchment tulip
cupcake liners 4 inches (10 cm) tall.

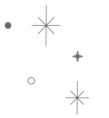

Recipe continues on the following page

continued from the previous page

Remove the dough from the refrigerator. On a lightly floured work surface, knock the dough back and divide it into 12 equal pieces. Shape each piece into a ball, place them in the paper molds or liners, and leave to rise in a warm, draft-free place for 1 hour. They will increase in size by about half.

Preheat the oven to 350°F (180°C). Lightly brush the top of each bread with beaten egg and sprinkle with the pearl sugar. Bake for about 15 minutes, then reduce the temperature to 300°F (150°C) and continue to bake until a skewer inserted into the center of a few test breads comes out clean, 12–15 minutes. Check the breads periodically, as the sugar and butter in the dough can cause them to brown too much before they are fully baked. If they are turning too dark, tent them loosely with aluminum foil. When they are ready, let cool on wire racks. Serve warm or at room temperature.

✳ CHEF'S NOTE

Italian 00 flour gives these panettone an especially soft, silky texture. It's a finely ground flour traditionally used for making pasta and pizza dough and is available from Italian markets and well-stocked supermarkets. Bread flour (UK strong white bread flour) can be substituted, but it will produce a slightly heavier, denser result.

Pearl sugar, also known as nib or nibbed sugar, is available in well-stocked supermarkets and from specialty baking suppliers. The large round crystals add a wonderful crunchy texture and festive "snowy" appearance to baked goods.

Ricotta Pancakes with Warm Blackberries and Caramelized Walnuts

These light-as-a-feather pancakes topped with unctuous blackberry compote and complemented by crunchy walnuts and creamy cinnamon cheese make a winter's breakfast fit for a king. If you like, garnish with fresh herbs.

FOR THE WALNUTS

2 tablespoons unsalted butter

¼ cup (50 g) superfine sugar

1 teaspoon ground cinnamon

20 walnut halves

FOR THE BLACKBERRY TOPPING

1¾ cups (250 g) fresh or frozen blackberries

¼ cup (50 g) superfine sugar

1 teaspoon fresh lemon juice

FOR THE CINNAMON CREAM CHEESE

7 oz (200 g) cream cheese, at room temperature

2 tablespoons plus 1 teaspoon superfine sugar

1 teaspoon ground cinnamon

FOR THE PANCAKES

1 cup (250 g) whole-milk ricotta cheese

¼ cup (50 g) superfine sugar

3 eggs, separated

Finely grated zest of 1 orange

1 teaspoon pure vanilla extract

2 tablespoons unsalted butter, melted, plus more butter for cooking

6½ tablespoons (50 g) brown spelt flour

Makes sixteen 4-inch (10-cm) pancakes; 4 servings

To prepare the walnuts, line a sheet pan with parchment paper or a silicone baking mat. In a heavy sauté pan, melt the butter with the sugar and cinnamon over medium heat. Stir to mix well, then cook gently for a couple of minutes until a light golden caramel forms. Add the walnuts to the pan and toss them to coat each one thoroughly in the caramel. Carefully transfer the nuts to the prepared sheet pan, spacing them out so they don't stick together. Set aside to cool and harden.

To make the blackberry topping, in a small saucepan, combine the blackberries, sugar, and lemon juice over low heat and cook, stirring occasionally, until the berries soften, 2–3 minutes. Then simmer gently to reduce the juices and thicken the mixture, 3–5 minutes. Remove from the heat, cover, and set aside.

To make the cinnamon cream cheese, in a small bowl, stir together the cream cheese, sugar, and cinnamon until thoroughly mixed. Cover and refrigerate until needed.

Recipe continues on the following page

continued from the previous page

To make the pancakes, preheat the oven to 250°F (120°C). In a large bowl, stir together the ricotta, sugar, and egg yolks until well mixed. Stir in the orange zest, vanilla, and butter, mixing well. Add the flour and mix just until incorporated. In a second large bowl, whisk the egg whites until stiff peaks form. Gently fold the egg whites into the ricotta mixture, being careful not to knock the air out.

Warm a large nonstick frying pan over medium heat, add 1 tablespoon butter, and swirl the pan to coat the bottom with the melting butter. Add a heaped tablespoon of the pancake batter and, using the back of the spoon, gently flatten it to a diameter of about 4 inches (10 cm). Add as many more pancakes as will fit without crowding. Cook until the tops rise and the undersides are golden, 1–2 minutes. Carefully flip the pancakes and cook on the second side until golden, 1–2 minutes. Transfer to a large sheet pan in a single layer and slip into the oven to keep warm while you cook the remaining batter the same way.

To serve, gently reheat the blackberry topping over low heat. For each serving, place a stack of pancakes on a warmed plate. Spoon one-fourth of the blackberries over the pancake stack, then scatter 5 walnut halves around the pancakes. Serve immediately. Pass the cinnamon cream cheese at the table.

SPICED CRANBERRY AND ORANGE GRANOLA

One of the many advantages of making this granola is the festive aroma of warming spice blended with vanilla and orange that fills the house as it bakes—so enticing. Topped with a generous dollop of Greek yogurt and a scattering of pomegranate seeds, it makes a wholesome start to a day of indulgence.

1½ cups (150 g) old-fashioned rolled oats

1 cup (200 g) steel-cut (jumbo) oats

½ cup (50 g) pecans

½ cup (50 g) pistachios

⅓ cup (50 g) flaxseeds

⅓ cup plus 1 tablespoon (50 g) pumpkin seeds (pepitas)

2½ tablespoons chia seeds

⅔ cup (150 ml) maple syrup

⅔ cup (150 g) coconut oil, melted

1 teaspoon pure vanilla extract

2 teaspoons mixed spice (see Chef's Note)

Finely grated zest of 1 orange

½ teaspoon salt

¾ cup plus 1 tablespoon (100 g) unsweetened dried cranberries

3 tablespoons cacao nibs

MAKES 15 SERVINGS

Position 2 oven racks in the center of the oven and preheat the oven to 350°F (180°C). Line 2 large sheet pans with parchment paper or silicone baking mats.

In a large bowl, combine the rolled and steel-cut oats, pecans, pistachios, flaxseeds, pumpkin seeds, and chia seeds and mix well. In a jug, mix together the maple syrup, coconut oil, vanilla, mixed spice, orange zest, and salt. Pour over the oat mixture and toss to coat the dry ingredients evenly.

Divide the granola mixture evenly between the prepared sheet pans, spreading it in an even layer. Bake for 15 minutes. Remove from the oven, divide the cranberries and cacao nibs evenly between the pans, and toss to mix evenly and to ensure the granola bakes evenly. Return the pans to the oven and bake until all the ingredients are lightly toasted, 10–15 minutes. Let cool completely on the pans.

Store in tightly capped jars or breakfast cereal containers. The granola will keep in a cool place for up to 2 weeks.

✳ CHEF'S NOTE

British mixed spice includes mace and coriander, making it a little less sweet and a bit more fragrant than the pumpkin pie spice sold in the United States.

Any combination of dried fruits, nuts, and seeds can be used as long as the proportions are kept the same. Apricots and macadamias in combination with cinnamon and clementine zest are also delicious.

SCRAMBLED EGG AND SMOKED SALMON PARCELS

You can't beat this classic combination: soft, creamy scrambled egg with a top note of chile enveloped in luxurious smoked salmon and served with zesty crème fraîche and crunchy brioche fingers.

14 oz (400 g) thinly sliced smoked salmon

8 extra-large eggs

2 tablespoons heavy cream

1 tablespoon finely chopped fresh chives

Salt and freshly ground black pepper

Pinch of freshly ground dried chile

1½ tablespoons butter

¼ cup (55 g) crème fraîche

Finely grated zest of 2 lemons

Handful of mustard greens and cress or fresh herbs

4 thick slices brioche, toasted, buttered, and cut into fingers

1 lemon, cut into 4 wedges

MAKES 4 SERVINGS

Preheat the broiler. Line 4 ramekins, each about 2¾ inches (7 cm) wide by 2 inches (2.5 cm) deep, with the smoked salmon, allowing the slices to overhang the rim (the overhang will be used to cover the top of the filled ramekin). Make sure there are no gaps.

In a bowl, whisk together the eggs, cream, and chives and season with salt and pepper and the ground chile. In a heavy, nonstick frying pan or saucepan, melt the butter over low heat. Add the egg mixture and cook, stirring constantly with a wooden spoon. When the eggs are nearly set, divide them evenly among the prepared ramekins. Fold the overhanging salmon over the egg to complete the parcels.

Carefully turn the parcels out of the ramekins onto warmed heatproof plates and place briefly under the broiler just to warm the salmon.

Serve each parcel with a dollop of crème fraîche topped with lemon zest, a scattering of mustard greens and cress or herbs, fingers of toasted brioche, and a lemon wedge.

STACKED TURKEY AND SMOKED HAM SANDWICH WITH CRANBERRY SAUCE

This substantial sandwich is stacked high with many of the classic flavors of Christmas. For those wanting something lighter—but equally festive—replace the bread with a corn tortilla for a delicious seasonal wrap.

2 tablespoons mayonnaise

1 teaspoon whole-grain mustard

¼ ripe avocado, peeled and sliced lengthwise

½ teaspoon fresh lemon juice

Fine sea salt and freshly ground black pepper

2 slices whole-wheat sourdough bread, toasted

Generous handful of mixed microgreens or arugula

2 thin slices roast turkey

2 tablespoons cranberry sauce

6 red and yellow cherry or grape tomatoes, sliced

¼ carrot, peeled and shaved into ribbons with a vegetable peeler

1 wafer-thin slice Gruyère cheese

2 thin slices smoked ham

1 tablespoon unsweetened dried cranberries

1 tablespoon walnut pieces

MAKES 1 SANDWICH

In a small bowl, stir together the mayonnaise and mustard. Put the avocado in a second small bowl, sprinkle with the lemon juice, season with salt and pepper, and toss gently to coat evenly.

To assemble the sandwich, put a slice of the toasted bread on a plate. Spread half of the mayonnaise-mustard mixture on the bread slice. Top with about one-third of the microgreens and half of the avocado. Fold the turkey slices in half, lay them on top of the avocado, and drizzle with the cranberry sauce. Follow this with a layer of half each of the tomatoes and carrot ribbons, the remaining avocado, half of the remaining microgreens, and then the Gruyère. Fold the ham slices in half and add them to the sandwich. Finish with the remaining tomatoes, carrots, and microgreens. Spread the second bread slice with the remaining mayonnaise-mustard mixture and place it, spread side down, on top of the sandwich.

Sprinkle the dried cranberries and walnuts around the sandwich. Serve immediately.

Tomato and Goat Cheese Mini Frittatas with Crushed Avocado

These quick-and-easy mini frittatas can be made up to 2 days in advance and reheated under the broiler. You can also use Christmas leftovers to make frittatas. Ham, pea, and ricotta and turkey, leek, and Parmesan are two mouthwatering combinations, especially when served with Tomato and Sweet Red Pepper Relish (page 150).

1 tablespoon olive oil, plus more for the muffin pan

24 mixed red and yellow cherry tomatoes

1 red bell pepper, seeded and diced

1 orange bell pepper, seeded and diced

Fine sea salt and freshly ground black pepper

1 teaspoon sugar

8 eggs

¼ cup plus 2½ tablespoons (100 ml) heavy cream

Handful of fresh basil leaves, torn, plus 1 tablespoon finely shredded leaves

5½ oz (150 g) fresh goat cheese from a small log, cut into ⅜-inch (1-cm) cubes

3 ripe avocados

Juice of ½ lemon

6 handfuls of small salad leaves or microgreens for garnish

Makes six 4-inch (10-cm) frittatas; 6 servings

Preheat the oven to 350°F (180°C). Oil 6 jumbo muffin-pan cups. Cut 12 parchment paper strips, each ¾ inch (2 cm) wide and 8 inches (20 cm) long. Using 2 strips per cup, arrange them in a cross, with the ends overlapping the rim (for easy removal of the frittatas).

In a large frying pan, heat the oil over high heat. Add the tomatoes and the red and orange peppers, season with salt and pepper and the sugar, and toss together until the tomato skins split and the peppers soften, about 2 minutes. Remove from the heat. In a bowl, whisk together the eggs and cream until blended and season with salt and pepper.

Divide the tomatoes and peppers evenly among the prepared muffin cups, layering them with the torn basil leaves and goat cheese. Pour the egg mixture over the top, dividing it evenly.

Bake the frittatas until set and golden on top, 15–20 minutes.

While the frittatas are baking, halve, pit, and peel the avocados and drop them into a bowl. Add the shredded basil and lemon juice, season with salt and pepper, and crush with a fork, mixing well.

When the frittatas are ready, using the parchment strips, carefully lift them from the pan. Serve warm with the crushed avocado on the side and a scattering of salad leaves.

WINDSOR CASTLE

Children's Treats

Christmas is an enchanting time of the year for children, but little ones haven't always been at the heart of the festivities. We have Prince Albert to thank for bringing some of today's best-loved Christmas traditions to Britain. He was intent on making it a magical time for children, and he is attributed with introducing indoor decorated Christmas trees, a custom that originated in Germany, where he was born. Perhaps Prince Albert would have enjoyed the edible Lemon Star Christmas Tree in this chapter.

During the twenty years that Queen Victoria and Prince Albert were together, they spent every Christmas at Windsor Castle, the eleventh-century royal residence in Berkshire. A press report from 1848 describes "gilt gingerbread . . . suspended by variously coloured ribbons from the branches [of the Christmas tree] at Windsor Castle," suggesting that this may be something else that Albert popularized. The Gingerbread Man Wreaths and the Mini Gingerbread Village in the pages that follow would have fit perfectly into a Victorian Christmas spread.

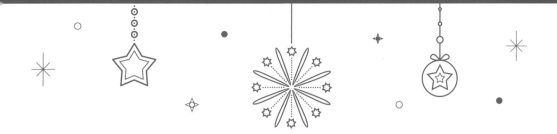

Queen Victoria's chef, Charles Elmé Francatelli, noted that "meringues while being baked must remain soft underneath" and recommended splashing the cooking surface with water prior to adding the lining paper and meringue mix. This instruction seems bizarre, but in the Victorian era, meringues were baked on wooden boards, so it does make sense. But do not try this when making the Meringue Snowflakes with your children!

GINGERBREAD MAN WREATHS

These are a delightful alternative to the nonedible variety! Gingerbread wreaths can be made in all shapes and sizes; star, heart, leaf, angel, and Christmas tree shapes work as well as the gingerbread man used here. You can also use a combination of shapes and sizes, sprinkles and sparkles, to create your own design.

FOR THE GINGERBREAD
½ cup plus 1 tablespoon (125 g) butter, at room temperature

½ cup (100 g) firmly packed light brown sugar

⅔ cup (200 g) golden syrup

2¾ cups (350 g) flour, plus more for the work surface

1 teaspoon baking soda

2 teaspoons ground ginger

1 teaspoon ground cinnamon

FOR THE ICING
1⅔ cups (200 g) confectioners' sugar, sifted

1 egg white

1 teaspoon fresh lemon juice

Pinch of salt

FOR THE DECORATION
Selection of cake decorations in festive colors

Red and/or green ribbon

MAKES 3 WREATHS, ONE 12 INCH (30 CM), ONE 8 INCH (20 CM), AND ONE 5½ INCH (14 CM)

Cut sheets of parchment paper to line 2 large sheet pans. Draw a 12-inch (30-cm) circle on the center of 1 sheet, then draw an 8-inch (20-cm) circle and a 5½-inch (14-cm) circle on the second sheet, spacing them well apart. Line the pans with the parchment, turning the parchment circles-side-down.

To make the gingerbread, in a food processor, combine the butter and sugar and process until smooth and creamy. Add the golden syrup, flour, baking soda, ginger, and cinnamon and process until the mixture is the texture of coarse bread crumbs. Tip into a large bowl and bring together by hand to form a smooth dough.

On a lightly floured work surface, roll out the dough ¼ inch (6 mm) thick. Using gingerbread man cutters, cut out shapes. To make the 12-inch (30-cm) wreath, you will need about eighteen 3-inch (7.5-cm) gingerbread men. To make the 8-inch (20-cm) wreath, you will need about fourteen 2½-inch (6-cm) gingerbread men. To make the 5½-inch (14-cm) wreath, you will need about twelve 1½-inch (4-cm) gingerbread men. If unable to cut out all the shapes you need, gather up the scraps, press together, roll out the dough, and cut out more shapes as needed.

To form the wreaths, using the circles on the parchment, arrange the gingerbread men with their heads touching the outside of the circle and with their hands and feet slightly overlapping. Chill for 20 minutes before baking. Meanwhile, preheat the oven to 300°F (150°C).

Bake the wreaths for 12–24 minutes, depending on their size (the smaller wreaths will bake more quickly). They are done when they are golden and still soft to the touch. Let cool completely on the pans on wire racks, then transfer the wreaths to the racks before decorating.

Recipe continues on the following page

continued from the previous page

While the wreaths are cooling, make the icing. In a bowl, using an electric mixer, beat together the confectioners' sugar, egg white, lemon juice, and salt on high speed until light and fluffy, 4–5 minutes.

Spoon the icing into a piping bag fitted with a ¹⁄₁₆-inch (2-mm) plain tip. Decorate the gingerbread men by piping faces onto them and then piping a vertical row of dots onto their bodies. Stick colored balls onto the body dots for buttons and onto the features as desired. Then pipe on any other features you like, such as feet, hands, hair, or even clothing.

Leave the icing to harden for about 30 minutes, then tie a length of ribbon around each wreath—making a single loop or multiple loops—to use for hanging.

Store the wreaths in an airtight container until ready to hang them. Otherwise, the gingerbread will lose its crispness in a day or two, especially if the weather is damp.

LEMON STAR CHRISTMAS TREE

To get this tree to stand tall and straight is a feat of culinary engineering, making it a wonderful family project. Decorating a small edible tree is every bit as much fun as dressing the real Christmas tree, but patience and a steady hand are required, as putting tiny sprinkles in just the right places is intricate work. The star-shaped biscuits are crisp, buttery, and delicious, but can you bear to deconstruct the tree to eat one?

FOR THE BISCUITS

1⅓ cups (300 g) butter, at room temperature

1¼ cups (240 g) superfine sugar

2 eggs, lightly beaten

2 teaspoons pure vanilla extract

½ teaspoon pure lemon oil

2 lemons

4 cups (500 g) flour, plus more for the work surface

FOR THE ICING

2½ cups (300 g) confectioners' sugar, sifted, plus more for dusting the tree

2–3 tablespoons fresh lemon juice

FOR THE DECORATION

Selection of cake decorations in festive colors (see Chef's Note)

MAKES 1 TREE, ABOUT
12 INCHES (30 CM) TALL

Position 2 oven racks in the center of the oven and preheat the oven to 300°F (150°C). Line 4 large sheet pans with parchment paper or silicone baking mats.

To make the biscuits, in a food processor, combine the butter and superfine sugar and process until smooth and creamy. Add the eggs, vanilla, and lemon oil, then finely grate the zest of both lemons directly into the processor bowl. Pulse the mixture a couple of times just to mix, then add the flour and process until the mixture is the texture of coarse bread crumbs. Tip into a large bowl and bring together by hand to form a smooth dough.

Divide the dough in half. On a lightly floured work surface, roll out half of the dough at a time ¼ inch (6 mm) thick. Using a set of star-shaped cutters, cut out 3 stars in each of the following sizes: 1⅓ inches (3.5 cm), 2 inches (5 cm), 2½ inches (6.5 cm), 3 inches (7.5 cm), 3¾ inches (9.5 cm), 4⅓ inches (11 cm), 4¾ inches (12 cm), 5⅓ inches (13.5 cm), and 6 inches (15 cm). Any other set of star cutters in roughly the same size and number can be used. To make a taller tree, also cut out thirty 1-inch (2.5-cm) plain circles, for placing between the stars when stacking the layers. Transfer the cutouts to the prepared pans, spacing them about 1 inch (2.5 cm) apart. Gather up the scraps, press them together, roll out the dough, and cut out more stars or circles as needed.

Recipe continues on the following page

continued from the previous page

Place 2 sheet pans in the oven and bake the biscuits, switching the pans between the racks and rotating the pans back to front halfway through baking, until they are pale golden, 6–12 minutes. (The smaller stars will take less time.) Transfer the biscuits to wire racks and let cool completely. Repeat with the remaining 2 sheet pans.

To make the icing, in a bowl, using a wooden spoon or an electric mixer, beat together the confectioners' sugar and 2 tablespoons of the lemon juice until smooth, adding more lemon juice if needed to achieve a good piping consistency. Spoon the icing into a piping bag fitted with a ⅛-inch (3-mm) plain tip.

To assemble the tree, have ready a large, flat plate. You will stack the stars from largest to smallest, rotating each one slightly so the points of each star alternate with the points of the star below. For a taller tree, insert a small circle biscuit after each star. To secure the layers, pipe a small amount of icing onto a layer before topping it. Stack 6 layers at a time, letting them stand for a few minutes to set and firm up before continuing to build the tree. If you like, top the tree with a small standing star, securing it in place with icing.

Once the tree is completed, drizzle the "branches" with the remaining icing and add the decorations. Dust the tree lightly with confectioners' sugar.

Store the tree under a glass dome or carefully wrapped in aluminum foil at room temperature. It will keep for 3–5 days.

✳ CHEF'S NOTE

The tree can be decorated with finely diced colorful glacé fruits and nuts instead of cake decorations.

Little individual trees, made by assembling a short stack of small stars, make a lovely edible gift or can be used as table decorations.

SUGAR MICE

One of my fondest childhood memories is of searching the top of my Christmas stocking for the little, characterful sugar mouse that I knew would be nestled there, one that had been lovingly crafted by my mother. This rather quirky British Christmas tradition is one that dates back to Victorian times. The sugar paste in this recipe is easy to prepare, but shaping the mice can be challenging and is always the cause of much hilarity in our house.

1 egg white

1 teaspoon fresh lemon juice

3¾ cups (350–450 g) confectioners' sugar, sifted, plus more for the work surface

Natural pink food coloring

Colored sugar balls for eyes and noses

4 red (strawberry) or black (licorice) sugar laces for tails

MAKES TWELVE $2\frac{1}{2}$–3-INCH (6–7.5-CM) MICE

In a bowl, using a balloon whisk, whisk the egg white until foamy. Add the lemon juice and whisk just to blend. Gradually add the sugar while mixing with a wooden spoon to form a stiff sugar paste. Divide the mixture in half. Put half into a second bowl and work a few drops of food coloring into it until it is evenly light pink. Leave the other half white.

Have ready wire racks to hold the mice. Lightly dust a work surface with sugar. Break off a piece of sugar paste the size of a large walnut and roll it into a cone shape on the sugared surface. Then flatten one side so the mouse will sit without rolling over. Close to the narrow end—about one-third of the way along—pinch out little ears and then pinch to make a nose. Press the sugar balls into the face for eyes and a nose and then press a 4-inch (10-cm) length of sugar lace into the rounded end of the mouse for a tail. Set the mouse on a wire rack. Repeat to use all the pink and white sugar paste.

Let the mice dry on the racks at room temperature for 12 hours. They will keep in an airtight container at room temperature for up to 3 weeks.

＊CHEF'S NOTE

You can add a few drops of pure peppermint oil to the sugar paste before dividing it in half. It helps to temper the sweetness.

'Twas the night before Christmas
When all through the house
Not a creature was stirring
Not even a mouse; . . .

—from *The Night Before Christmas*
by Clement Clarke Moore, first published 1823

MERINGUE SNOWFLAKES

For a very festive children's dessert, serve these snowflakes with vanilla ice cream and red and green fruit-flavored gelatin. They are fun to make and decorate (no matter what your age), but I find that children are never happier than when armed with a piping bag full of meringue! You can draw templates on the parchment paper used for lining the sheet pans to use as a guide to piping, or you can make free-form snowflakes.

FOR THE MERINGUE

1¼ cups (250 g) superfine sugar

½ cup (120 g) egg whites
(from 4–5 eggs)

½ teaspoon fresh lemon juice

FOR THE DECORATION

Selection of sprinkles in gold, silver, blue, and white

Pearl sugar (see Chef's Note, page 16)

MAKES ABOUT TWELVE 3–4-INCH
(7.5–10-CM) SNOWFLAKES

Position 2 oven racks in the center of the oven and preheat the oven to 400°F (200°C). Line 2 large sheet pans with parchment paper or silicone baking mats. If you want to make all the snowflakes a similar size, trace 4-inch (10-cm) circles on the parchment. Turn the parchment over before piping the meringues to avoid getting ink on them.

To make the meringue, spread the sugar in a thin, even layer on a prepared sheet pan and place it in the oven for 5 minutes. Meanwhile, in a stand mixer fitted with the whip attachment, beat the egg whites on medium-high speed until stiff peaks form.

Remove the sugar from the oven and reduce the temperature to 250°F (120°C). With the mixer running on high speed, add the sugar a spoonful at a time, beating after each addition, until the meringue comes back up to stiff peaks. Once all the sugar is incorporated, add the lemon juice and continue to beat for 3–5 minutes. The meringue is ready to use if it forms smooth, shiny peaks when the whip attachment is lifted out of it.

Divide the meringue between 2 piping bags, one fitted with a ¼-inch (6-mm) plain tip and the other with a ¼-inch (6-mm) star tip. Pipe variations of symmetrical hexagonal shapes onto the prepared sheet pans to create snowflakes. Start with a six-point shape and then add further detail. If the snowflakes are too small and the lines are too fine, they will be too fragile. Snowflakes of about 4 inches (10 cm) are a good size for a child to manage piping. They will expand slightly when baking, so if you have not drawn templates, leave a little space between them. Decorate with sprinkles and pearl sugar.

Bake the snowflakes, switching the pans between the racks and rotating them back to front at the halfway point, until they are completely dry, 30–40 minutes. They should remain bright white during baking, without the slightest hint of color. Let cool completely on the pans on wire racks. Once cool, remove them very carefully, as they can break easily. To store, layer them with bubble wrap (to prevent breakage) in large airtight containers. They will keep at room temperature for up to 1 week.

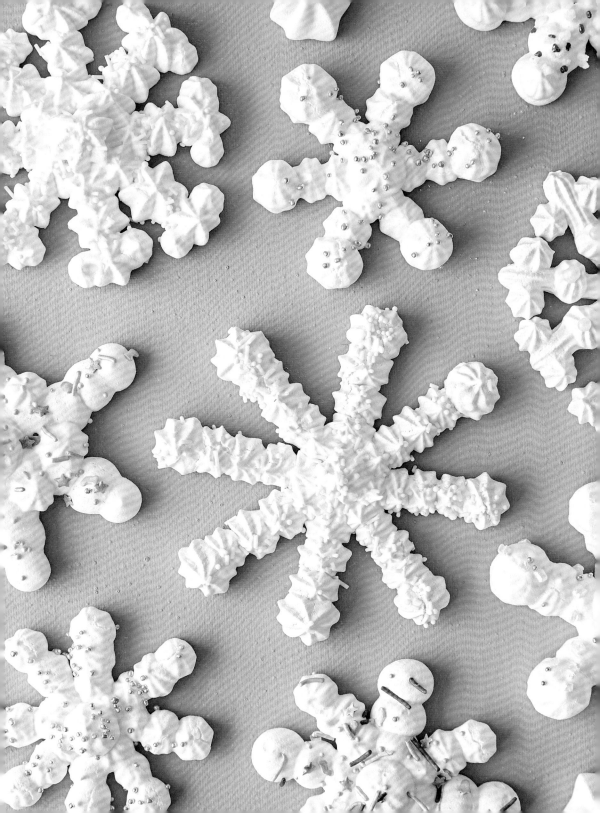

MARSHMALLOW SNOWMEN

These easy, festive snowmen are made by threading small, medium, or giant marshmallows onto wooden skewers. Children always enjoy styling their snowmen with fancy hats and brightly colored scarves and buttons.

FOR EACH SNOWMAN

3 marshmallows, in the size of choice

1 wooden skewer

1 roll fruit leather or jelly strip for the scarf and hat band

Icing (see Mini Gingerbread Village, page 44)

½ Cadbury chocolate mini roll or 1 medium marshmallow and 1 biscuit (cookie) for the hat (see Chef's Note)

Colored sugar balls and/or gelatin-based chewable candies for the eyes, nose, and buttons

Sprinkles if making marshmallow hat

1 biscuit (cookie) for base (optional)

MAKES 1 SNOWMAN

To assemble each snowman, thread 3 marshmallows onto the skewer. Alternatively, stack the marshmallows. Make a scarf by wrapping the fruit leather around the stacked marshmallows, positioning it between the top and middle marshmallow, and securing it with a little icing.

Make the hat by sticking the half mini roll, cut side down, onto the center of the biscuit and using a little icing to secure the mini roll in place. If you like, add a hat band made of fruit leather. Alternatively, spread the top of the biscuit and the top and sides of the medium marshmallow with icing, set the bottom of the marshmallow on the center of the biscuit, pressing gently so it adheres, and then coat the top of the biscuit and the marshmallow with sprinkles. Leave the hat to dry before sticking it to the top of the head with a blob of icing.

To finish, attach sugar balls for the eyes, nose, and buttons, using the icing as glue.

If you want to create a base for your snowman, generously spread a biscuit with icing and stand your snowman on the biscuit, pressing gently so it adheres.

Repeat the process to make as many snowmen as you like.

✳ CHEF'S NOTE

An inverted peanut butter cup can be used as an alternative to the chocolate mini roll or the marshmallow hat.

If you don't have icing left over from making gingerbread houses, make a smaller batch of the icing using 1 egg white, 1¾ cups (200 g) confectioners' sugar, and ¾ teaspoon fresh lemon juice.

MINI GINGERBREAD VILLAGE

Gingerbread houses are magical through the eyes of a child. Creating this miniature winter wonderland of tiny houses, chalets, and snowy log piles evokes the spirit of Christmas for young and old alike. Assembling it can be a little fiddly, but a small gingerbread house is a lot easier to construct than a large one, as it is much lighter and the roof is a lot less likely to slide off!

FOR THE GINGERBREAD

6⅓ cups (800 g) flour, plus more for the work surface

¾ cup (160 g) firmly packed light brown sugar

1 teaspoon ground ginger

1 teaspoon baking soda

1 cup plus 2½ tablespoons (260 g) butter, melted and cooled

⅔ cup (200 g) golden syrup

FOR THE ICING

5½ cups (650 g) confectioners' sugar, sifted

3 egg whites

2 teaspoons fresh lemon juice

FOR THE DECORATION

Tiny silver, gold, and white sugar balls

Sprinkles

Confectioners' sugar for dusting

Pearl sugar (see Chef's Note, page 16), optional

4 small battery-powered tealights (optional)

Fresh rosemary sprigs

MAKES 4 SMALL HOUSES

To make the gingerbread, preheat the oven to 350°F (180°C). Line 3 large sheet pans with parchment paper or silicone baking mats.

In a food processor, combine the flour, brown sugar, ginger, and baking soda and pulse a few times to mix. Add the butter and golden syrup and process until the mixture is the texture of coarse bread crumbs. Tip into a large bowl and bring together by hand to form a smooth dough.

Divide the dough into thirds. On a lightly floured work surface, roll out one-third of the dough into a rectangle ¼-inch (8-mm) thick to fit a prepared sheet pan. Transfer the dough to the pan. Bake until golden, 12–15 minutes. Repeat with the remaining dough portions, baking them one at a time.

As soon as the first pan of gingerbread comes out of the oven, lay the gingerbread house templates (see next spread) on top and, using a small, sharp knife and a metal ruler, cut out all the pieces, leaving them on the sheet pan until they are cold and firm. Repeat with the remaining 2 pans, working carefully to make sure you cut out all the pieces you will need. (See Chef's Note.)

To make the icing, in a large bowl, using an electric mixer, beat together the sugar, egg whites, and lemon juice on high speed until light and fluffy, 3–4 minutes. Divide about half of the icing between 2 piping bags, one fitted with a ¹⁄₁₆-inch (2-mm) plain tip and the other with a small star tip.

Lay all the gingerbread pieces on wire racks to cool completely. Once the gingerbread pieces are cool, decorate as desired. For example, using the plain piping tip, outline the doors and windows, and pipe tiles onto the roof pieces. Use the star tip for any other decoration on the houses. Add sugar balls and sprinkles to decorate the pieces while the icing is still soft so they will adhere.

To assemble each house, start with the front panel. Using the plain tip, pipe a stripe of icing down each side on the back. Secure the 2 side panels to the front and hold for a few moments while the icing starts to set. Repeat with the back section of the house. Once again, hold it together for a few moments to set. Now pipe along the edges of the roof pieces and secure them to the house, holding each one in position for a few minutes so it doesn't slip off. Repeat to make 3 more houses. Let each house stand undisturbed for at least 30 minutes before moving it.

To finish, spread the remaining icing on a flat white plate at least 12 inches (30 cm) in diameter or an attractive rustic wooden board, covering it completely. Dust generously with confectioners' sugar and/or sprinkle with pearl sugar to simulate snow. Position the houses on the snowy base as you like. Slip a tealight inside each house if possible, to give a cozy glow through the windows. Using rosemary sprigs, create trees, and using offcuts of the gingerbread, make small piles of logs and stepping stones. Finally, add a light dusting of confectioners' sugar to the "village." While the gingerbread will look good for several weeks, it is best eaten within 1 week.

✳ CHEF'S NOTE

Extra gingerbread trimmings can be used in the White Chocolate Tiffin recipe on page 124. They can also be crushed and used in a crumb crust for a tart.

To include a snowman in your village, mold a small amount of white fondant into a snowman shape, create a hat by topping a chocolate button with an M&M or similar candy, and then decorate as you like.

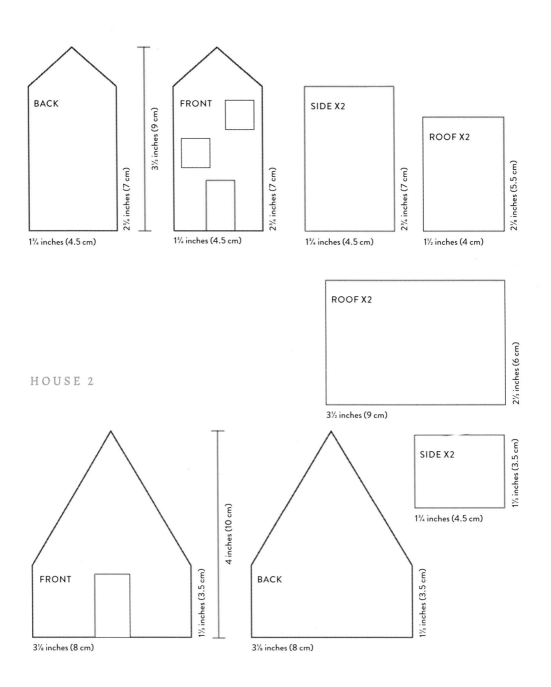

BACK

FRONT

SIDE X2

ROOF X2

3½ inches (9 cm)

2¾ inches (7 cm)

2¾ inches (7 cm)

2¾ inches (7 cm)

2⅛ inches (5.5 cm)

1¾ inches (4.5 cm)

1¾ inches (4.5 cm)

1¾ inches (4.5 cm)

1½ inches (4 cm)

ROOF X2

2⅓ inches (6 cm)

3½ inches (9 cm)

HOUSE 2

SIDE X2

1⅓ inches (3.5 cm)

1¾ inches (4.5 cm)

FRONT

BACK

4 inches (10 cm)

1⅓ inches (3.5 cm)

1⅓ inches (3.5 cm)

3⅛ inches (8 cm)

3⅛ inches (8 cm)

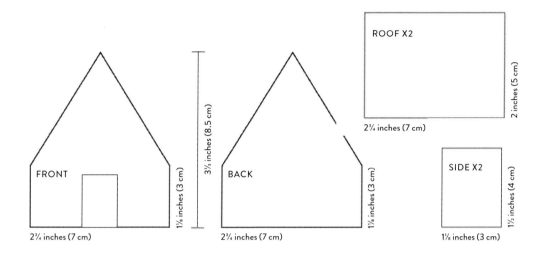

FRONT

2¾ inches (7 cm)

1⅛ inches (3 cm)

3⅓ inches (8.5 cm)

BACK

2¾ inches (7 cm)

1⅛ inches (3 cm)

ROOF X2

2¾ inches (7 cm)

2 inches (5 cm)

SIDE X2

1⅛ inches (3 cm)

1½ inches (4 cm)

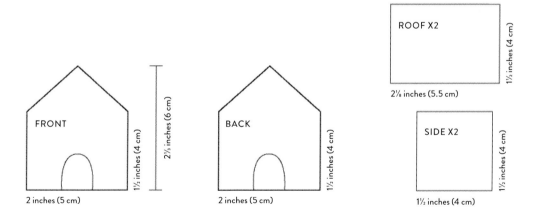

FRONT

2 inches (5 cm)

1½ inches (4 cm)

2⅓ inches (6 cm)

BACK

2 inches (5 cm)

1½ inches (4 cm)

ROOF X2

2⅛ inches (5.5 cm)

1½ inches (4 cm)

SIDE X2

1½ inches (4 cm)

1½ inches (4 cm)

EDINBURGH CASTLE

Festive Drinks

A royal residence since the twelfth century, Edinburgh Castle stands high up on Castle Rock, proudly presiding over the city below. It is spectacular and supremely atmospheric, particularly around Christmastime and Hogmanay (New Year's Eve in Scotland), when it forms the backdrop to much merrymaking. Scotland produces some of the world's finest whiskies, so it is not surprising that locals traditionally keep the cold at bay at times such as this by enjoying a "wee dram" or two. Indeed, Edinburgh Castle even produces its own ten-year-old single malt.

In 1566, Mary, Queen of Scots, who at the time was wed to Henry Stuart (Lord Darnley), gave birth to the future James VI of Scotland (James I of England and Ireland) at the castle. In his late fifties, the king developed a severe illness, and the royal physicians regularly administered him herbal poultices and other remedies. Acting without the consent of the king's physicians, the Duke of Buckingham, James's confidant and court favorite, is said to have given the king a special cordial—a medieval concoction of alcohol, spices, and herbs designed to target the illness. The king's health reportedly began to deteriorate rapidly after receiving it and he refused to continue drinking it. He died not long after, and rumors of poisoning abounded.

This chapter is filled with warming and festive drinks for one and all, and while I wouldn't recommend enhancing your cordial as was done in James's time, do experiment with new ingredients, just as the Stuarts did, and you are sure to create all manner of stimulating seasonal concoctions!

SCOTCH COFFEE

This is a Scottish twist on the well-known after-dinner drink Irish coffee. In Scotch coffee, the Irish whiskey is replaced by Drambuie, which is a blend of Scotch whisky, heather honey, herbs, and spices. It marries beautifully with the freshly brewed coffee and brown sugar. The layer of lightly whipped cream that floats on top envelops every sip in a rich, velvety mantle—it is divine!

1¾ fl oz (50 ml) Drambuie

1–2 teaspoons Demerara sugar

7 fl oz (200 ml) hot freshly brewed coffee

⅔ cup (160 ml) very lightly whipped heavy cream

Edible small gold stars or grated dark chocolate for decorating

MAKES 1 SERVING

Preheat a 9–fl oz (250-ml) stemmed glass by placing a teaspoon into it and then filling it with boiling or very hot water. (The teaspoon will prevent the glass from cracking.) After about 1 minute, tip the water out. Add the Drambuie, the sugar to taste, and then the coffee and give everything a good stir.

Carefully pour the cream over the back of a tablespoon held just above the hot coffee. The spoon ensures the cream won't break the surface of the coffee and sink to the bottom. Sprinkle with gold stars and serve immediately.

MINTED BERRY CORDIAL

This cordial embodies the spirit of summer, whatever time of year it is drunk. Served over ice in a tall glass, it makes a wonderfully cooling and refreshing drink. However, if presented steaming hot in a mug, it is a great winter-warmer for children and adults alike. You can also splash a little into your favorite cocktail for a dash of color and a burst of fresh berry flavor.

18 oz (500 g) mixed fresh berries, such as raspberries, blueberries, red currants, and black currants (about 3½ cups)

4½ cups (900 g) sugar

1 lemon, sliced

Handful of fresh mint leaves

2 teaspoons tartaric acid (see Chef's Note)

2 cups (475 ml) boiling water

MAKES ABOUT 6½ CUPS (1.5 L)

In a large heatproof bowl, combine the berries, sugar, lemon, mint, and tartaric acid. Pour the boiling water over the mixture. Then, using a balloon whisk, mix everything together until the sugar has dissolved. Let cool to room temperature.

Cover the bowl with a plate and place it in the refrigerator for 5 days. Once a day, remove the bowl, stir the mixture well, re-cover, and return it to the refrigerator.

Sterilize two 26-fl oz (750-ml) heatproof bottles (see Chef's Note, page 145). Pour the berry mixture through a fine-mesh sieve into a large saucepan. Bring to a boil over medium heat, skimming off any impurities that rise to the surface. Remove from the heat.

Line the sieve with a double thickness of cheesecloth and strain the hot mixture through the sieve into a heatproof jug. Then, using a funnel, divide the mixture between the sterilized bottles. Let cool completely, then cap tightly. An unopened bottle of the cordial will keep in the refrigerator for up to 6 months. Once a bottle is opened, it will keep for up to 4 weeks.

To serve the cordial, dilute 1 part cordial with 3–4 parts chilled water, according to taste. You can use still or sparkling water and add ice, a lemon wedge, and a fresh mint sprig to each glass. To serve the cordial hot, dilute 1 part cordial with 3–4 parts boiling water and omit the garnish.

✳ CHEF'S NOTE

Tartaric acid is a preservative. It is an organic natural acid that occurs in many fruits, most notably in grapes. It is available online and in some well-stocked supermarkets and in shops carrying winemaking supplies.

DOM PEDRO

This South African classic of vanilla ice cream blended with heavy cream and whisky is halfway between a dessert and a cocktail—a kind of grown-up milkshake. A young chef traveling through Scotland is said to have drenched his vanilla ice cream with his whisky during a long lunch at a distillery, sowing the seed for the creation of the Dom Pedro upon his return to his restaurant in South Africa.

1 oz (30 g) dark chocolate, melted

3–4 scoops good-quality vanilla ice cream

3½ tablespoons (50 ml) heavy cream

3½ tablespoons (50 ml) high-quality Scotch whisky

Christmas sprinkles for decorating

MAKES 1 SERVING

Drizzle the melted chocolate down the inside of a tall stemmed glass, turning the glass as you work to create a random pattern on the sides.

In a blender, combine the ice cream, heavy cream, and whisky and blend until smooth.

Carefully pour the ice cream mixture into the glass and top with sprinkles. Serve immediately.

＊CHEF'S NOTE

The Scotch whisky can be replaced by Baileys Irish Cream, Frangelico, Kahlúa, or Amarula.

You can use chocolate or caramel sauce in place of the melted chocolate on the inside of the glass.

WARM SPICED APPLE AND POMEGRANATE JUICE

Serve this delightfully aromatic and warming drink as an alcohol-free alternative to mulled wine. It is important to use a good-quality apple juice made from freshly pressed apples rather than one made from concentrate.

1 quart (1 l) apple juice

1 cup (240 ml) pomegranate juice

8 whole cloves

1 cinnamon stick, 2 inches (5 cm) long

1 small tangerine, unpeeled, thinly sliced

Zest of 1 small lime, in long strips ⅜ inch (1 cm) wide

½ vanilla bean, split lengthwise

1–2 tablespoons light brown sugar

Quartered tangerine slices, fresh thyme sprigs, and 6 cinnamon sticks, each 4–6 inches (10–15 cm) long, for serving (optional)

MAKES 6 SERVINGS

In a heavy saucepan, combine the apple juice, pomegranate juice, cloves, cinnamon stick, tangerine, lime zest, vanilla bean, and the sugar to taste, depending on how sweet the apple juice is. Place over medium heat, bring slowly to the simmering point, cover, and cook for 1 minute. Remove from the heat and let stand for at least 20 minutes to allow the flavors to develop.

Strain through a fine-mesh sieve and then reheat before pouring into a clear-glass jug or directly into individual glasses. Garnish each glass with small pieces of tangerine, a thyme sprig, and a cinnamon stick "stirrer," if using. All of these give off a wonderful aroma. Serve immediately.

BAILEYS HOT CHOCOLATE WITH MARSHMALLOW SNOWMAN

This is a deliciously indulgent—and wonderfully whimsical—adult Christmas treat. You can also serve it without the Baileys to young connoisseurs. Making the snowmen is a great project for children, and they love topping the hot chocolate with the "squirty" cream!

1 cup (240 ml) whole or low-fat milk

Favorite hot chocolate powder to make 1 cup (240 ml)

Pinch of ground cinnamon

¼ teaspoon pure vanilla extract

3½ tablespoons (50 ml) Baileys Irish Cream

1 Marshmallow Snowman (page 41), made with medium marshmallows

Aerosol whipped cream for topping

MAKES 1 SERVING

In a small saucepan, combine the milk, chocolate powder, and cinnamon. Place over medium heat and bring to a simmer while whisking constantly with a balloon whisk. Whisk in the vanilla and Baileys, then remove from the heat and pour into a large cup or mug.

Position the snowman in the cup, top the chocolate with a generous amount of whipped cream, and serve immediately.

> ✳ CHEF'S NOTE
>
> I find that using aerosol whipped cream is more successful than topping the hot chocolate with homemade whipped cream, which dissolves and sinks quite quickly.

"FLEURISSIMO" CHAMPAGNE COCKTAIL

This simple floral cocktail was created in honor of Princess Grace of Monaco. The rose petal cradling a blueberry is a particularly elegant and eye-catching garnish. It makes the cocktail wonderfully festive and befitting any Christmas celebration.

1 white sugar cube

5 dashes of Peychaud's bitters

⅙ fl oz (5 ml) violet liqueur

½ fl oz (15 ml) XO Cognac

About 5 fl oz (150 ml) Champagne

A red rose petal and a blueberry for garnish

MAKES 1 SERVING

Grasp the sugar cube with tongs and slowly drip the bitters onto it. Carefully place the sugar cube on the bottom of a champagne flute.

Add the violet liqueur and Cognac and top up with the Champagne. Float the rose petal on the surface of the Champagne and delicately place the blueberry onto the petal. Serve immediately.

MULLED WINE WITH CLEMENTINES, CLOVES, AND JUNIPER

This recipe is only a guide. Mulled wine should be made to your taste, and thus all the ingredients and quantities here can be adjusted accordingly. Also, you don't need to purchase an expensive wine. Modestly priced Merlot, Zinfandel, and Garnacha are good choices, as they are fruity and full bodied and can support all the flavors that are being added.

1 bottle (750 ml) fruity red wine

1 cinnamon stick, about 2 inches (5 cm) long

6 juniper berries

4 whole cloves

2 bay leaves

Zest of 1 lemon, in long strips ⅜ inch (1 cm) wide

1 clementine or blood orange, unpeeled, thinly sliced

¼ cup (80 g) raw honey

Handful of fresh cranberries for decorating (optional)

MAKES 4–5 SERVINGS

In a large saucepan, combine the wine, cinnamon stick, juniper berries, cloves, bay leaves, lemon zest, clementine, and honey. Over medium heat, stir to dissolve the honey and bring to a gentle simmer, about 2 minutes. Remove from the heat and let stand for about 20 minutes to allow the flavors to develop.

Before serving, reheat gently. Do not allow to boil. Strain through a fine-mesh sieve into a heatproof jug.

WILD STRAWBERRY AND RED CURRANT CHAMPAGNE COCKTAIL

This celebratory Champagne cocktail was created by legendary mixologist Salvatore Calabrese. It takes a little practice to create the split colors, but the final effect is well worth the effort. Crème de cassis (black currant liqueur) can be substituted for the fraise des bois (wild strawberry) liqueur.

3 fresh stems red currants, frozen

1 tablespoon superfine sugar

½ fl oz (15 ml) cranberry juice

2 dashes fresh lemon juice

½–1 fl oz (15–30 ml) fraise des bois liqueur

1 fl oz (30 ml) vodka

3½ fl oz (100 ml) Champagne, chilled

MAKES 1 SERVING

Put 2 of the red currant stems and the sugar in a bowl and muddle with a wooden spoon to release the juice. Add the cranberry juice, lemon juice, liqueur, and vodka and stir well. Strain through a fine-mesh sieve into a small glass container, cover tightly, and chill well.

To serve, pour the chilled red currant mixture into a champagne flute. Very slowly pour the Champagne into the flute. Be sure to work slowly so the Champagne does not break through the red currant layer. Garnish the glass with the remaining stem of frozen red currants, draping it over the rim. Serve immediately.

HAMPTON
COURT PALACE

Edible Gifts

Hampton Court Palace, in southwest London, was famously home to Henry VIII, whose yuletide celebrations were legendary. Food has a long legacy of being gifted at Christmas, particularly luxury items. We are told that Pope Julius II once sent Henry VIII a hundred wheels of Parmesan, a little of which would surely have been enjoyed with some British cheese during the festive season. The blue cheese and walnut biscuits in this chapter would no doubt have sat very comfortably alongside the pope's extravagant gift!

Salt was a valuable commodity in the Tudor era. The French king, Francis I, sent a "clock salt" to Henry VIII as a diplomatic gift. It was a glittering bejeweled object that was both table clock and salt cellar, and most importantly, it was a status symbol. The closer a diner was seated to the clock salt, the higher the person's status. Today, salt is less valued as a commodity, however the range of artisanal salts available is impressive. The flavored salts in this chapter, prepared with quality flaked sea salt, make creative culinary gifts.

In December 1899, Queen Victoria popularized the tradition of giving chocolate as a Christmas gift when she sent specially commissioned boxed chocolates to the British troops fighting the Boer War in South Africa. However, two hundred years before that, in the 1690s, it was William III and Queen Mary who had engaged

a royal chocolate maker and built a customized chocolate kitchen at Hampton Court.

For lovers of white chocolate, the fudge with raspberries and macadamias makes a noble gift, while the large chocolate biscotti laced with cherries and pistachios are perfect for aficionados of dark chocolate.

This elaborate object, which is both a timepiece and a salt dispenser, was made by Pierre Mangot, goldsmith to the French court, in the 1530s.

White Chocolate, Raspberry, and Macadamia Fudge

Traditionally fudge needs to be boiled for some time, and testing to see if it is ready can be tricky. This recipe doesn't require any boiling, so it is safe and quick for children to make. The result is a softer fudge and one that should be kept chilled, but it is no less satisfying. Individually wrapped bars of fudge are perfect to slip into the top of a Christmas stocking.

1 can (14 fl oz/425 ml) sweetened condensed milk

1 tablespoon raspberry liqueur, such as Chambord

1 teaspoon pure vanilla extract

18 oz (500 g) white chocolate, chopped

2½ tablespoons unsalted butter, cubed

½ cup plus 1 tablespoon (80 g) macadamia nuts, toasted

2 tablespoons freeze-dried raspberry powder, plus more for dusting

2 tablespoons freeze-dried raspberry pieces, plus more for sprinkling

Makes thirty-six 1¼-inch (3-cm) squares or six 7 x 1¼-inch (18 x 3-cm) bars

Line the bottom and sides of a 7-inch (18-cm) square baking pan with plastic wrap. Let the plastic wrap overhang the sides so the fudge block can be lifted out of the pan for easier cutting.

Pour the condensed milk into a large heatproof bowl and stir in the liqueur and vanilla, followed by the chocolate and butter. Place the bowl over (not touching) simmering water in a saucepan and stir constantly until the chocolate and butter are melted. Take care not to let the mixture get too hot or it will split (become lumpy). Continue to stir until the mixture is thick, creamy, and homogenous. Alternatively, microwave the mixture on medium power for 30 seconds, take it out and stir it, and then repeat the process two or three more times until the mixture is the correct consistency.

Sprinkle the macadamias and the raspberry powder and pieces into the bowl and, using a heat-resistant rubber spatula, mix them in until evenly distributed. Quickly transfer the mixture to the prepared pan and smooth the surface with a palette knife or offset spatula. Dust the top with raspberry powder and sprinkle with raspberry pieces. Let cool for 30 minutes, then cover and refrigerate until set, about 2 hours.

When the fudge is firm, using the overhanging plastic wrap, lift out the block of fudge and place on a cutting board. Cut into 36 squares or 6 bars. The fudge will keep in an airtight container in the refrigerator for up to 2 weeks.

✳ CHEF'S NOTE

Crème de cassis can be used instead of raspberry liqueur, or the alcohol can be omitted. Likewise, almonds can replace the macadamias, or you can leave out the nuts.

BRAMBLE VODKA

If foraging in the hedgerows in the autumn leaves you with a glut of blackberries, pop some into a large jar with some sugar, a split vanilla bean or two, and your favorite vodka. Shake it up every few days, and by Christmastime, you will have fantastic bramble-infused vodka. I recommend using one of the Swedish vodka brands.

Generous 2 cups (300 g) fresh or frozen blackberries

1 cup (200 g) superfine sugar

2 vanilla beans, split lengthwise

3 cups (700 ml) vodka, preferably Swedish

MAKES ABOUT 1 QUART (1 L)

Sterilize a 1-quart (1-l) canning jar (see Chef's Note, page 145).

Put the berries into a colander or sieve and rinse under running cool water. Drain well and dry thoroughly on paper towels. Tip the berries into the canning jar, sprinkle with the sugar, add the vanilla beans, and pour the vodka over the top. Seal the jar and shake to dissolve the sugar.

Leave the jar in a cool, dark place for 3 months, shaking it every few days. After this time, strain the mixture through a fine-mesh sieve into a clean container. Then, for a clear and sparkling result, line the sieve with a double thickness of cheesecloth and strain the liquid into a jug.

Pour the vodka into as many small, attractive bottles as you like, cap tightly, and then label them for the lucky recipients and include the recipe for a bramble vodka cocktail (see Chef's Note).

✳ CHEF'S NOTE

To make a bramble vodka cocktail, put 3 blackberries and 1 teaspoon superfine sugar into a tumbler and crush them together with a fork. Squeeze in the juice of $\frac{1}{4}$ lime and add 4 ice cubes. Pour $1\frac{3}{4}$ fl oz (50 ml) Bramble Vodka over the ice, then fill the glass almost to the top with chilled soda water. Strip some of the leaves off a fresh rosemary sprig, thread a couple of blackberries and thin lime wedges onto the stem, and balance the sprig across the top of the glass. Serve at once.

SPICED NUT MIX

A little spicy, a little salty, and with a hint of sweetness, these delightfully crunchy, very moreish nuts go perfectly with Christmas drinks. Packed in an attractive jar or bag, they make a lovely edible gift. The choice of nuts can be varied according to your preference, and the quantity of chile flakes can be increased to make them more fiery.

¼ cup (60 ml) maple syrup

1 tablespoon walnut oil

½ teaspoon smoked or plain paprika

½ teaspoon red chile flakes

½ teaspoon ground cumin

1½ teaspoons flaked sea salt

1 cup (100 g) pecan halves

1 cup (100 g) whole cashews

⅓ cup (50 g) whole Brazil nuts

⅓ cup (50 g) whole macadamia nuts

⅓ cup (50 g) pumpkin seeds (pepitas)

Few fresh thyme or rosemary sprigs (optional)

MAKES ABOUT 1 QUART (1 L)

Preheat the oven to 325°F (165°C). Line a large sheet pan with parchment paper or a silicone baking mat.

In a large bowl, stir together the maple syrup, oil, paprika, chile flakes, cumin, and salt, mixing well. Tip the pecans, cashews, Brazil nuts, macadamias, and pumpkin seeds into the bowl and toss them with the maple syrup mixture until they are all thoroughly coated in the spicy glaze.

Pour the nuts onto the prepared sheet pan and spread them in an even layer. Add the thyme sprigs, if using, spacing them out around the pan. Bake for 5 minutes, then remove the pan from the oven, stir the nuts so they will cook evenly (this also helps to coat them evenly in the glaze), and return the pan to the oven. Repeat this process of baking for 5 minutes and stirring an additional three or four times. The nuts are ready when they are a little darker in color, have formed small clumps, and all the glaze has dried.

Remove the pan from the oven and stir the nuts one more time, spreading them in an even layer. You can leave some of the nuts in small clumps, if you like. Allow to cool completely before packing them into a gift box, bag, or jar for gifting. They will keep in an airtight container at room temperature for up to 2 months.

SAVORY BLUE CHEESE AND WALNUT BISCUITS

Paired with a wedge of artisanal cheese and a jar of Tomato and Sweet Red Pepper Relish (page 150) or Spicy Pear Chutney (page 151), these biscuits make an enviable Christmas gift. They are the ultimate accompaniment to any cheese board.

1 cup (125 g) flour, plus more for the work surface

4 tablespoons (60 g) cold butter, diced

3 oz (90 g) blue cheese, crumbled

½ cup (60 g) walnuts, chopped

1 egg, separated

Leaves from 5 fresh thyme sprigs

Flaked sea salt for sprinkling

MAKES ABOUT THIRTY 2-INCH (5-CM) BISCUITS

Preheat the oven to 350°F (180°C). Line 2 sheet pans with parchment paper or silicone baking mats.

In a food processor, combine the flour and butter and pulse until the mixture resembles coarse bread crumbs. Add 2 oz (60 g) of the cheese, ¼ cup (30 g) of the walnuts, and the egg yolk and process just until the dough begins to come together. Tip into a bowl and bring together by hand to form a smooth, pliable dough.

On a lightly floured work surface, roll out the dough ¼ inch (6 mm) thick. Using a 2-inch (5-cm) cutter in the shape of your choice, cut out as many biscuits as possible. Transfer the cutouts to the prepared sheet pans, spacing them about 1 inch (2.5 cm) apart. Gather up the scraps, press them together, reroll the dough, cut out more biscuits, and add them to the pans.

In a small bowl, mix together the remaining cheese and walnuts and the thyme leaves. In a second small bowl, lightly beat the egg white. Lightly brush the biscuits with the egg white, then scatter the cheese mixture on the biscuits. Finish each biscuit with a few flakes of salt.

Bake the biscuits until golden, 15–20 minutes. Let cool completely on the pans on wire racks before packing into boxes for gifting. The biscuits will keep in an airtight container at room temperature for up to 5 days. If needed, they can be re-crisped in a 350°F (180°C) oven for a few minutes.

✳ CHEF'S NOTE

The stronger the cheese, the more delicious the biscuits will be. Stilton makes particularly wonderful biscuits.

Flavored Salts

Flavored salt is a great gift for budding home chefs. It secretly and subtly elevates everyday dishes to something special. It is important to use good-quality flaked sea salt, as it seasons and adds flavor to a dish without overpowering the taste of the food. Do not use iodized table salt for these mixtures, as it will mask delicate flavors. See the Chef's Note on page 145 for directions on sterilizing the jars. The flavored salts will keep at room temperature for up to 1 year.

Each recipe makes one $\frac{1}{2}$-pint (240-ml) jar

LEMON AND THYME SALT

Use this salt to season fish, chicken, and turkey. It is also great in risotto, on new potatoes, and in hollandaise sauce.

3 lemons

Leaves from 3 fresh thyme sprigs

1 cup (120 g) flaked sea salt

Preheat the oven to 200°F (95°C). Line a small sheet pan with parchment paper.

Finely grate the zest from 2 of the lemons. Using a vegetable peeler, remove the zest from the third lemon in long strips. Spread all the lemon zest and the thyme leaves on the prepared sheet pan. Place in the oven until crisp and all the moisture has evaporated, about 30 minutes. Let cool completely.

In a small bowl, combine the dried lemon zest and thyme and the salt and mix well. Pack into a sterilized jar and cap tightly.

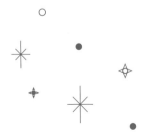

PINK PEPPERCORN AND ROSEMARY SALT

I like to top homemade focaccia with a sprinkle of this salt and a drizzle of olive oil before it goes into the oven to bake. It is also wonderful paired with plenty of garlic for roast lamb.

Leaves from 3 fresh rosemary sprigs
1 cup (120 g) flaked sea salt
4 teaspoons pink peppercorns

Preheat the oven to 200°F (95°C). Line a small sheet pan with parchment paper. Spread the rosemary leaves on the prepared pan and place in the oven until crisp and all the moisture has evaporated, about 30 minutes. Let cool completely.

In a small bowl, combine the dried rosemary, salt, and peppercorns and mix well. Pack into a sterilized jar and cap tightly.

VANILLA SALT

The sweet-savory flavor profile of this salt is amazing in such homemade confections as fudge, toffee, truffles, and caramels. You can also sprinkle it sparingly on brownies, shortbread, or chocolate-caramel tartlets; use it in cheesecake; or add a pinch to a mug of hot cocoa.

1 cup (120 g) flaked sea salt
1 teaspoon vanilla powder
⅓ vanilla bean, halved lengthwise

In a small bowl, combine the salt, vanilla powder, and vanilla bean and mix well. Pack into a sterilized jar and cap tightly.

RED CHILE SALT

The chile flakes give this salt some heat, and the sweet red pepper flakes add a lot of color without adding any fire. Use the salt on grilled meats or add a pinch or two to an omelet or a simple pasta dish.

1 cup (120 g) flaked sea salt
2 teaspoons sweet red pepper flakes
1 teaspoon red chile flakes
½ teaspoon smoked or plain paprika

In a small bowl, combine the salt, sweet pepper and chile flakes, and paprika and mix well. Pack into a sterilized jar and cap tightly.

Giant Chocolate, Cherry, and Pistachio Biscotti

Serve these biscotti alongside a mug of hot chocolate, coffee, or even Scotch Coffee (page 53). They are a wonderful marriage of tart cherries, creamy pistachios, and slightly bitter cacao nibs wrapped up in a not-too-sweet, not-too-crunchy biscuit. To cap a festive meal, serve a giant biscotto with a scoop of chocolate or pistachio ice cream and a scoop of cherry sorbet.

2 cups plus 2 tablespoons (260 g) flour, plus more for the work surface

¾ cup (150 g) superfine sugar

½ cup (40 g) unsweetened cocoa powder

1½ teaspoons baking powder

3 eggs, lightly beaten

2 teaspoons pure vanilla extract

⅔ cup (100 g) plump dried cherries

½ cup (60 g) pistachios

1 tablespoon cacao nibs

MAKES ABOUT TWENTY-EIGHT 8-INCH (20-CM) BISCOTTI

✳ CHEF'S NOTE

Dried cranberries, dark or golden raisins, or dried currants that have been macerated in rum, brandy, or Marsala can be substituted for the cherries.

The biscotti can be made in any size. Mini biscotti go well with a demitasse of coffee at the end of a meal.

Preheat the oven to 325°F (165°C). Line 2 large sheet pans with parchment paper or silicone baking mats.

In a large bowl, sift together the flour, sugar, cocoa powder, and baking powder. Add the eggs, vanilla, cherries, pistachios, and cacao nibs and mix with a wooden spoon until a smooth dough forms.

Turn the dough out onto a lightly floured surface and knead until smooth and no longer sticky. Divide the mixture in half and shape each half into a log 8 inches (20 cm) long and 3–4 inches (7.5–10 cm) wide. Flatten each log slightly to give it a symmetrical shape, then transfer each log to a prepared sheet pan.

Bake the logs until firm to the touch, 25–30 minutes. Let cool for about 5 minutes on the pans on wire racks. Leave the oven on.

Transfer the logs to a cutting board. Using a large, sharp serrated knife, slice each log lengthwise into biscotti ¼ inch (6 mm) thick. Each log should yield about 14 biscotti. Carefully lay them, not touching, on the sheet pans. Return the biscotti to the oven until crisp, 5–10 minutes. Be careful not to overbake them at this stage, or the pistachios will lose their brilliant green color.

Transfer the biscotti to a wire rack and let cool completely before gift wrapping in a tall jar, box, or eco-cellophane bag tied with ribbon. They will keep in an airtight container at room temperature for up to 2 weeks.

OSBORNE HOUSE

Afternoon Tea

Osborne House was the much-loved seaside home and holiday retreat of Queen Victoria and Prince Albert. It is located in East Cowes, on the Isle of Wight, and has stunning views across the Solent, which are said to have reminded Prince Albert of the Bay of Naples. Fittingly, he designed the house, which he had built in the mid-1800s, in the style of an Italian Renaissance palazzo.

It was during Queen Victoria's reign that afternoon tea came into being. The Duchess of Bedford, who was one of the queen's ladies-in-waiting, is credited with having the idea of serving something small between lunch and dinner to stave off the pangs of hunger, a custom that evolved into one of our finest British traditions. When at Osborne House, the queen regularly took her afternoon tea on the lawns, and undoubtedly her namesake Victoria sandwich cake would have been served.

The opera singer Dame Emma Albani Gye was a friend of Queen Victoria's, and she talked about intimate afternoon teas spent in the queen's company drinking black tea, which the queen very much enjoyed, and eating bread and butter and cake. This is in stark contrast to the more commonly presented image of large plates

bulging with sandwiches, pastries, and cakes and to the frequent references to Queen Victoria's insatiable appetite for all things sweet, like the quote from her art tutor (and renowned "nonsense poet") Edward Lear, who noted in one of his humorous rhymes, that, "the Queen of England eats macaroon cakes continually."

Winter Berry and Walnut Victoria Sandwich

No afternoon tea is complete without a Victoria sandwich, particularly one that might take place at Osborne House, Queen Victoria's seaside retreat. The addition of toasted walnuts and brown sugar lends a superbly rich and velvety texture to the cake, while the colorful berry filling and decoration make it beautifully festive.

FOR THE CAKE

1½ cups (350 g) butter, at room temperature, plus more for the pans

1 cup (100 g) walnuts

2 cups (250 g) flour

1¼ cups (250 g) superfine sugar

½ cup (100 g) firmly packed light brown sugar

7 eggs

1 teaspoon pure vanilla extract

5 teaspoons baking powder

2 tablespoons milk

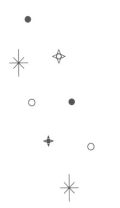

To make the cake, preheat the oven to 350°F (180°C). Line the bottom of three 8-inch (20-cm) round cake pans with parchment paper, then butter the paper and the sides of the pans.

Spread the walnuts on a sheet pan and toast in the oven until they are fragrant and deepen in color, 12–15 minutes. Pour onto a plate and let cool completely.

In a food processor, combine the nuts and a few spoonfuls of the flour and pulse until the nuts are finely ground. Add the remaining flour and process briefly to mix.

In a large bowl, using a handheld mixer, beat together the butter and both sugars on medium-high speed until light and fluffy. In a jug, lightly beat the eggs. With the mixer on medium speed, gradually add the eggs to the bowl, beating well after each addition. If the mixture starts to curdle, add a couple of tablespoons of the flour mixture. When all the eggs are incorporated, add the vanilla, baking powder, and the remaining flour mixture and mix with a large metal spoon until incorporated. Finish with the milk, mixing just until the batter is smooth.

Divide the batter evenly among the prepared cake pans. Smooth the tops with a palette knife or offset spatula and make a small indent in the center of each layer so the top is flat rather than peaked when the cake emerges from the oven.

Recipe continues on the following page

continued from the previous page

FOR THE FILLING

1⅓ cups (200 g) fresh or frozen blackberries

2 tablespoons firmly packed light brown sugar

⅔ cup (200 g) black currant jam

1 cup plus 2 tablespoons (250 g) mascarpone

¾ cup plus 2 tablespoons (200 ml) heavy cream

1 teaspoon pure vanilla extract

2 tablespoons superfine sugar

FOR THE DECORATION

1⅓ cups (200 g) mixed fresh or frozen berries, such as blackberries and red currants, and cherries, thawed and patted dry if frozen

Few fresh rosemary or thyme sprigs

Confectioners' sugar for dusting

MAKES 10 SERVINGS

Bake the cakes until golden and the tops spring back to a light touch, 18–20 minutes. Turn the cakes out onto wire racks, peel off the parchment, turn upright, and let cool completely.

While the cakes are in the oven, make the filling. In a small saucepan, combine the blackberries, brown sugar, and 2 tablespoons of the jam and cook over low heat, stirring gently to dissolve the sugar, just until the berries soften, 3–4 minutes. The berries should remain whole. Set aside to cool. In a medium bowl, using the mixer, beat together the mascarpone, cream, vanilla, and superfine sugar on low speed until the mixture holds its shape.

Before assembling the cake, make sure each cake layer has a flat top. Trim away any peak with a serrated knife. Place the first layer on a large, flat cake plate. Spread with half of the remaining jam, top with half of the mascarpone mixture and then with half of the cooled blackberries, spreading each addition evenly across the whole layer to the edges. Place the second cake layer on top and repeat the process, using the remaining jam, mascarpone mixture, and berries, then top with the third layer. Decorate with the mixed berries and cherries in a heap in the center along with the rosemary sprigs. Dust the top of the cake with confectioners' sugar.

Little Ginger Cakes with King's Ginger Frosting

These rich, moist ginger cakes are a fabulous alternative to the traditional Christmas fruitcake. The King's Ginger Liqueur in the frosting has an entirely royal pedigree; it became famous in the reign of Edward VII. At the request of the monarch's doctor, it was produced as a warming drink for the king to take after winter morning rides in his new "horseless carriage."

FOR THE CAKES

1¾ oz (50 g) crystallized ginger (about 4½ tablespoons)

2¾ oz (85 g) drained stem ginger in syrup (4 bulbs)

½ cup plus 2 teaspoons (125 g) butter

⅔ cup (200 g) golden syrup

3½ tablespoons (50 ml) syrup from the stem ginger

½ cup (100 g) firmly packed dark muscovado sugar

2 teaspoons ground ginger

1 teaspoon mixed spice (see Chef's Note, page 21)

Pinch of paprika or cayenne pepper

Pinch of fine sea salt

2 eggs

1 cup (240 ml) milk

1 cup plus 3½ tablespoons (150 g) all-purpose flour

⅔ cup (75 g) brown spelt flour

1 teaspoon baking soda

1 teaspoon baking powder

Preheat the oven to 325°F (165°C). Line the bottom and sides of fifteen 2½-inch (6-cm) straight-sided round molds with parchment paper. Alternatively, use standard muffin pans and line 15 cups with paper liners (though the gingerbread may stick to the liners, depending on their quality).

In a food processor, combine the crystallized and stem ginger and pulse until a smooth paste forms. Alternatively, grate both gingers on a fine-rasp grater. Transfer the gingers to a large, heavy pan and add the butter, both syrups, sugar, ground ginger, mixed spice, paprika, and salt. Warm gently over low heat until the butter melts, then stir until all the ingredients are well mixed. Do not allow to boil. In a small bowl, whisk together the eggs and milk until blended, then add to the pan and, using a large balloon whisk, mix until incorporated. Add both flours, the baking soda, and the baking powder and whisk together until smooth, making sure no small lumps of flour remain.

Divide the batter evenly among the prepared molds. Bake until a skewer inserted into the center of a few cakes comes out clean and the tops spring back to a light touch, 12–15 minutes. Invert the molds onto wire racks, lift off the molds, turn the cakes upright, and let cool completely. Do not remove the parchment until the cakes are at room temperature.

Recipe continues on the following page

continued from the previous page

FOR THE FROSTING

3½ tablespoons (50 g) butter, at room temperature

1¾ cups (200 g) confectioners' sugar

1 teaspoon King's Ginger Liqueur (see Chef's Note)

½ teaspoon pure vanilla extract

3½ tablespoons (50 g) cream cheese, at room temperature

FOR THE DECORATION

30–40 small gingerbread holly leaves (see Chef's Note)

Small red and silver or white balls

Confectioners' sugar for dusting

MAKES FIFTEEN 2½-INCH (6-CM) CAKES

To make the frosting, in a bowl, using a handheld mixer, beat the butter on medium speed until soft and light. Add the confectioners' sugar, liqueur, and vanilla and continue to beat until fluffy. Add the cream cheese and beat until light in color and texture.

To assemble and decorate the cakes, using a serrated knife, cut each one in half horizontally. Arrange the bottom halves, cut side up, on a work surface. Place a generous tablespoon of frosting in the center of a bottom half. Close with the top half, pressing down lightly to spread the frosting to the edges. Repeat with the remaining cakes. Divide the remaining frosting evenly among the tops of all the cakes and spread it to the edges. Decorate each cake with 2 or 3 gingerbread holly leaves and a few red balls for berries. Finish with silver balls, then lightly dust the cakes with confectioners' sugar before serving.

The cakes will keep in an airtight container in the refrigerator for up to 1 week.

✳ CHEF'S NOTE

To make the holly leaves, use the dough for the Gingerbread Man Wreaths on page 31. Make one quarter of the quantity in the recipe. Roll out the dough ¼ inch (6 mm) thick, cut out shapes with a small holly leaf–shaped cutter, and bake as directed for the smallest gingerbread men. It is best to decorate the cakes with the holly leaves just before serving, as they lose their crispness when in contact with the frosting. Alternatively, the cakes can be decorated with Christmas-themed sprinkles or left plain.

Brandy, fresh lemon juice, or pure vanilla extract can be substituted for the liqueur in the frosting. All of them marry well with ginger cake.

Unfrosted ginger cakes will keep in an airtight container at room temperature for up to 2 weeks. They become moister with age.

This recipe can also be baked in a 7-inch (18-cm) round cake pan with 4-inch (10-cm) sides. Increase the baking time to 30–35 minutes.

TEA SANDWICHES

This appealing selection of bite-size sandwiches is quick to make, and both the bread and the toppings can be varied according to the Christmas leftovers in your refrigerator.

GOAT CHEESE AND CRUSHED AVOCADO WITH LEMON AND MINT

2 slices brioche, each at least
4 inches (10 cm) square

½ large, ripe avocado, peeled

Juice and finely grated zest of
½ lemon

Fine sea salt and freshly ground
black pepper

2 tablespoons fresh goat cheese

8 tiny fresh mint sprigs or small
mint leaves for garnish (optional)

MAKES 8 SMALL OPEN-FACE
SANDWICHES

Using a 1½-inch (4-cm) plain round cutter, cut 4 circles from each brioche slice. In a small bowl, using a fork, crush the avocado with the lemon juice and season to taste with salt and pepper. Spoon the avocado onto the brioche circles, dividing it evenly, and top each avocado mound with an equal amount of the cheese. Garnish with the lemon zest and finish with a mint sprig (if using). Serve immediately.

> ✳ **CHEF'S NOTE**
>
> The brioche can be toasted, but it has a tendency to
> lose its crispness quickly, so if you prefer it toasted, the
> sandwiches must be eaten straightaway.

TURKEY, CRANBERRY SAUCE, WALNUTS, AND MICROGREENS

6 slices sprouted wheat bread, each
about 3 inches (7.5 cm) square and
⅜ inch (1 cm) thick, buttered

3 large slices smoked or plain turkey

2 tablespoons cranberry sauce

6 walnut halves

Handful of fine cress for garnish

MAKES 6 SMALL OPEN-FACE
SANDWICHES

Lay the bread slices, buttered side up, on a cutting board and trim off the crusts. Cut the turkey into 6 squares to fit the slices exactly. Divide the turkey trimmings evenly among the bread slices, then neatly top each with a square of turkey. Spoon a small dollop of cranberry sauce onto the center of each turkey square and top with a walnut and a couple of cress shoots. Serve immediately.

Recipes continue on the following page

continued from the previous page

SMOKED SALMON WITH CREAM CHEESE AND CUCUMBER

4 slices sprouted wheat bread, each about 3 inches (7.5 cm) square and ⅜ inch (1 cm) thick

4 tablespoons (60 g) cream cheese, at room temperature

1 oz (30 g) thinly sliced smoked salmon

Freshly ground black pepper

½ lemon

12 wafer-thin, skin-on cucumber slices

Microgreens for garnish

MAKES 6 SMALL SANDWICHES

Lay the bread slices on a cutting board and spread each one with some of the cream cheese, extending it right to the edges. Lay the smoked salmon on 2 of the slices, season with a few twists of black pepper and a few drops of juice from the lemon half, and then top with the remaining 2 bread slices, cream cheese side down. Spread the tops of both little sandwiches with more cream cheese and lay the cucumber slices on top of 1 sandwich. Place the second sandwich, cream cheese side down, on top of the cucumber and press together to form a neat stack. Using a sharp, serrated bread knife, trim off the crusts. Then cut the stack in half one way and in thirds the other way to yield 6 small sandwiches. Lay the sandwiches on a plate and scatter with a few microgreens.

The sandwiches will keep, well wrapped, in the refrigerator for up to 24 hours.

CHEDDAR AND VINE-RIPENED TOMATOES

2 large slices white sourdough bread, toasted

2 tablespoons good-quality basil pesto

¼ cup (30 g) finely grated sharp Cheddar cheese

1 tablespoon mayonnaise

8 assorted small vine-ripened tomatoes (preferably red, orange, yellow, and purple), thinly sliced (32 slices total)

Extra-virgin olive oil for finishing

Small fresh Greek and red basil sprigs for garnish

MAKES 8 SMALL OPEN-FACE SANDWICHES

Lay the bread slices on a cutting board. Spread each slice with an equal amount of the pesto, extending it to the edges. In a small bowl, stir together the cheese and mayonnaise. Spread half of the cheese mixture on each bread slice, extending it to the edges. Cut each bread slice into 4 equal strips, discarding the crusts at the edges. Lay 4 tomato slices on each strip and drizzle with a few drops of oil. Arrange on a plate and garnish with the basil. Serve immediately.

Raspberry-Almond Shortbread with Marzipan

The combination of buttery almond shortbread with tangy raspberry jam and marzipan is heavenly. You can make either dainty individual rounds or a slab of shortbread to cut into fingers. Apricot jam makes a delicious alternative to the raspberry jam.

FOR THE SHORTBREAD

½ cup plus 2 teaspoons (125 g) cold butter, plus more for the tartlet molds if using

1 cup (125 g) flour

⅓ cup plus 1 tablespoon (50 g) confectioners' sugar

½ cup (50 g) ground almonds

1 teaspoon pure vanilla extract

FOR THE TOPPING

Confectioners' sugar for dusting

5½ oz (150 g) marzipan

⅔ cup (200 g) raspberry jam

1 tablespoon sliced almonds (optional)

Makes 12 generous fingers or fifteen 2-inch (5-cm) rounds

To make the shortbread, line the bottom and sides of an 8-inch (20-cm) square baking pan with parchment paper, extending the parchment above the rim to use for lifting the baked shortbread from the pan, or line the bottom of fifteen 2-inch (5-cm) round tartlet molds with parchment paper and butter the sides.

In a food processor, combine the butter, flour, sugar, almonds, and vanilla and process until the dough is the texture of crumbs. Tip into a bowl and bring together by hand to form a smooth dough.

Press the dough evenly into the prepared square pan, using the back of a spoon to smooth it, or shape the dough into 15 equal-size balls and press each ball into a prepared round mold, bringing the dough up a little higher around the sides. Prick the dough lightly all over with a fork. Arrange the round molds on a large sheet pan. Chill the dough for 20 minutes. Preheat the oven to 325°F (165°C).

Bake the shortbread until light golden but still quite soft to the touch, about 20 minutes for the square pan and 8–12 minutes for the tartlet molds. Let cool in the pan or the molds on a wire rack.

Recipe continues on the following page

continued from the previous page

While the shortbread is baking, make the topping. Lightly dust a work surface or parchment paper with confectioners' sugar and roll out the marzipan about ¼ inch (6 mm) thick. For the large slab, cut out at least 15 small, medium, and large marzipan shapes using snowflake, star, or any other shaped cutters of your choice. For each small round, cut out 2–3 small marzipan shapes of choice. For tiny snowflakes, a plunger cutter works best. Keep the marzipan to one side.

Preheat the broiler. Using a palette knife or an offset spatula, spread the jam evenly over the top of the large cooled shortbread. If you have baked small rounds, spread a little jam in the center of each round. Position the marzipan shapes on top of the jam. Place the shortbread under the broiler and broil until the marzipan is golden brown, 8–10 minutes. If using the almonds, sprinkle them over the shortbread just before it is ready and return it to the broiler for 1 minute. Watch closely, as marzipan and almonds burn easily.

Let the shortbread cool completely on a wire rack, then carefully ease it out of the square pan or the round molds. Lightly dust with confectioners' sugar, then, if you have baked the slab, cut into 12 fingers to serve. The shortbread will keep in an airtight container at room temperature for up to 1 week.

BRANDY SNAPS FILLED WITH CHESTNUT CREAM AND CHOCOLATE CREAM

Brandy snaps have a reputation for being very tricky to make, but they really aren't. Be sure to use silicone baking mats to line the sheet pans so the brandy snaps bake evenly and are easy to lift off and roll up. They are delicious filled or left plain.

FOR THE BRANDY SNAPS
3½ tablespoons (50 g) butter

¼ cup (50 g) Demerara sugar

2½ tablespoons golden syrup

Finely grated zest of 1 lemon

½ teaspoon fresh lemon juice

2 teaspoons brandy

⅓ cup plus 1 tablespoon (50 g) flour

½ teaspoon ground ginger

FOR THE FILLINGS
⅓ cup plus 1½ tablespoons (100 g) chestnut puree

1 teaspoon pure vanilla extract

1 tablespoon brandy

1 tablespoon superfine sugar

7 tablespoons (100 g) mascarpone

1¾ oz (50 g) dark chocolate

MAKES 16 FILLED BISCUITS

To make the brandy snaps, preheat the oven to 325°F (165°C). Line 2 large sheet pans with silicone baking mats or parchment paper.

In a small, heavy saucepan, melt together the butter, Demerara sugar, and golden syrup over low heat and stir to mix well. Do not allow to boil. Remove from the heat and stir in the lemon zest and juice and brandy. Lastly, add the flour and ginger and mix well.

Spoon a tablespoonful of the batter onto a prepared sheet pan for each brandy snap, spreading out each spoonful with the back of the spoon to a round about 6 inches (15 cm) in diameter and spacing the rounds well apart. Form no more than 4 rounds on the sheet pan and load and bake only 1 pan at a time.

Bake until golden, 8–10 minutes. Remove from the oven and leave on the pan for about 30 seconds before, working quickly, loosening each brandy snap with a palette knife and rolling it around the handle of a wooden spoon, overlapping the edges, to form a cylinder. Once the brandy snaps have cooled a little and are firm, slide the spoon out carefully, place the brandy snap, seam side down, on a wire rack to cool, and repeat with the remaining rounds. If they become brittle before shaping, return them to the oven for a few moments. While the first batch is baking, get the second batch ready so you can slip it into the oven as soon as the first batch comes out. Repeat the whole process until all the batter has been baked, always allowing the pans to cool before adding batter to them.

To make the fillings, in a small bowl, using a wooden spoon, beat together the chestnut puree, vanilla, brandy, and superfine sugar until well mixed. Add half of the mascarpone and mix well. Keep this chestnut filling mixture to one side. To make the chocolate filling, melt the chocolate in a small heatproof bowl placed over (not touching) simmering water or in a microwave, let cool, and then mix with the remaining mascarpone until evenly incorporated.

To assemble, spoon each filling into a piping bag fitted with a ⅜-inch (1-cm) plain tip. Fill the brandy snaps by piping the filling in from both ends. Stack the filled brandy snaps on a plate and serve.

The unfilled brandy snaps will stay crisp in an airtight container at room temperature for up to 1 week. Once they are filled, they will start to soften within an hour.

CHOCOLATE-MINT YULE LOG

For every British child, a chocolate log is a very important part of a Christmas afternoon tea. Children love to help make, decorate, and eat it. The mint buttercream in this recipe adds a lovely splash of green inside the log, and the flavor is deliciously refreshing.

FOR THE CAKE

Butter for the pan

4 eggs

½ cup (100 g) superfine sugar, plus more for dusting

½ cup plus 1 tablespoon (70 g) flour

6 tablespoons (35 g) unsweetened cocoa powder

1 teaspoon baking powder

To make the cake, preheat the oven to 400°F (200°C). Lightly butter the bottom and sides of a 13 x 9-inch (33 x 23-cm) jelly roll (Swiss roll) pan with ¾–1-inch (2–2.5-cm) sides and line the bottom with parchment paper.

In a large bowl, using an electric mixer, beat together the eggs and superfine sugar on high speed until the mixture is pale in color, light, and frothy. Sift together the flour, cocoa powder, and baking powder into the bowl and, using a metal spoon, carefully cut and fold together until all the flour and cocoa are incorporated. Take care not to beat the air out of the batter.

Pour the batter into the prepared pan and, using an offset spatula or palette knife, spread it evenly, extending it into the corners. Bake the cake until well risen and firm to the touch, 8–10 minutes.

While the cake is baking, lay a damp kitchen towel flat on a work surface and top it with a piece of parchment paper that is slightly larger than the pan. Generously dust the parchment with superfine sugar.

When the cake is ready, remove the pan from the oven and carefully invert it onto the paper. Lift off the pan and gently peel the parchment from the bottom of the cake. Using a serrated knife, slightly trim the two short sides to remove any hard edges. Then, starting on one of the long sides, roll up the cake along with the sheet of parchment. Place seam-side-down on a wire rack and let cool completely.

Recipe continues on the following page

continued from the previous page

FOR THE BUTTERCREAM

⅔ cup (150 g) butter, at room temperature

3 cups (300 g) sifted confectioners' sugar

6–10 drops pure peppermint oil

3–4 tablespoons milk

Few drops natural green food coloring

⅓ cup (30 g) unsweetened cocoa powder

FOR THE DECORATION

Fresh holly leaves and herb sprigs, such as thyme and/or rosemary

Red sugar balls

Confectioners' sugar for dusting

M AKES 8 SERVINGS

✳ CHEF'S NOTE

The filling can be varied. Use chocolate or vanilla buttercream or, for a more indulgent treat, fill with fresh whipped cream and well-drained tinned cherries.

While the cake is cooling, make the buttercream. In a medium bowl, using the electric mixer, beat the butter on medium speed for about 1 minute to soften it, then add the confectioners' sugar and the peppermint oil to taste and continue to beat until light and creamy, 3–4 minutes. Beat in 1 tablespoon of the milk. Transfer ⅔ cup (200 g) of the buttercream to a second medium bowl. Add a couple of drops of the food coloring to the second bowl and beat on medium speed until the color is evenly distributed and the buttercream is light and creamy, adding an additional drop or two of coloring if needed to achieve a shade you like. Keep to one side. To the original bowl of buttercream, add the cocoa powder and 1–2 tablespoons milk and beat on medium speed until light and creamy and the cocoa is evenly distributed, adding more milk if needed to achieve a good consistency.

Uncurl the cold cake roll and remove the parchment. Using a palette knife, spread the green mint buttercream evenly on the cake, extending it to the edges, and then reroll the cake, creating a firm roll.

Cut off one-fourth of the cake, making the cut on the diagonal. Transfer the large piece of cake to a serving plate. Position the angled end of the small piece against the large piece to simulate a branch.

Using a small palette knife, spread the chocolate buttercream over the cake, covering it completely, including the ends, and creating a slightly rough effect to simulate bark. Decorate with holly leaves, herb sprigs, and red sugar balls, then lightly dust with confectioners' sugar.

The yule log will keep in an airtight container in the refrigerator for up to 5 days.

St. James's Palace

Nibbles and Savories

In the 1530s, Henry VIII ordered the building of St. James's Palace on the site of a one-time hospital dedicated to Saint James the Less. Located in the City of Westminster in London, it was the residence of the kings and queens of England for over three hundred years, until the reign of Queen Victoria. Today, the palace is home to several members of the royal family and their household offices and is the site of scores of receptions each year for charities associated with family members and for visiting dignitaries.

The recipes in the pages that follow offer inspiration for simple nibbles to enjoy with a celebratory Christmas drink. From the festive twist on the universally loved sausage roll and the child-friendly skewers of tomato, basil, and mozzarella to the sophistication of shots of creamy celeriac soup with hazelnuts, there is something for all ages and tastes.

Celeriac wasn't introduced to Britain until the 1700s, but if it had been around in Tudor times, when St. James's Palace was first occupied, it would have made a very fine pottage, a staple early soup made from vegetables and grains. What distinguished a pottage of the wealthy from that of the poorer classes would often be the addition of spices or chopped nuts, so the hazelnuts must surely "socially elevate" the celeriac soup in this chapter!

CREAMY CELERIAC SOUP WITH TOASTED HAZELNUTS

One shot of this soup is never enough! The rich flavor and velvety texture, punctuated by crunchy hazelnut pieces, make it irresistible. The use of oat milk in this recipe makes it suitable for vegans.

1 celeriac (celery root), about 1 lb (450 g), peeled and cut into ⅜-inch (1-cm) cubes

1 yellow onion, finely chopped

1 clove garlic, crushed

2 fresh thyme sprigs

1 tablespoon olive oil

2¼ cups (525 ml) vegetable stock, heated to a simmer

¾ cup plus 2 tablespoons (200 ml) oat milk

Fine sea salt and freshly ground black pepper

1 tablespoon very finely chopped fresh chives

2 tablespoons finely chopped toasted hazelnuts

2 tablespoons hazelnut oil

MAKES ABOUT TWELVE ⅓-CUP (80-ML) SERVINGS

In a heavy-bottomed saucepan, combine the celeriac, onion, garlic, thyme, and olive oil over medium heat and cook, stirring occasionally, until the onion is translucent and the celeriac is beginning to soften, 8–10 minutes. Add the hot stock, cover, and simmer over medium heat until the celeriac is very tender and starting to break down, about 25 minutes.

Remove from the heat, remove and discard the thyme sprigs, and stir in the oat milk. Transfer to a blender and blend until smooth, thick, and velvety. Season to taste with salt and pepper.

When ready to serve, pour the soup into a clean saucepan and reheat over medium heat until piping hot. Transfer to warmed demitasse cups or small tumblers, filling to within ⅜ inch (1 cm) of the rim. Sprinkle with the chives and hazelnuts and drizzle with a little hazelnut oil. Serve immediately.

Pancetta-Wrapped Vegetable Bundles

Made with batons of carrot and parsnip, these multicolored bundles make a cheerful addition to a selection of hors d'oeuvres for a holiday cocktail party and are also hearty enough to accompany a Christmas roast. To make a vegetarian bundle, use strips of cooked leek in place of the pancetta. The little bundles can be assembled a day in advance and roasted just before serving.

6 medium-size carrots, 2 orange, 2 yellow, and 2 purple

2 medium-size parsnips

1 tablespoon maple syrup

1 tablespoon balsamic vinegar

1 teaspoon whole-grain mustard

1 tablespoon extra-virgin olive oil, plus more for the sheet pan

Fine sea salt and freshly ground black pepper

8 thin slices pancetta, halved

Leaves from 2 fresh thyme sprigs

MAKES ABOUT 16 BUNDLES

Peel the carrots and parsnips and cut them into batons 2½ inches (6 cm) long by ¼ inch (6 mm) thick. You should have 32 batons of parsnip and of each type of carrot.

Bring a large saucepan of salted water to a boil over high heat. Tip the vegetable batons into the boiling water and cook for a minute or two. They should be barely tender. Drain thoroughly and return to the pan.

In a small bowl, whisk together the maple syrup, vinegar, mustard, and oil and season with salt and pepper. Pour over the vegetable batons, toss to coat, and then cook over low heat, stirring often, for a few minutes until the batons are glazed with the dressing.

Preheat the oven to 350°F (180°C). Brush a large sheet pan with oil.

To make up each bundle, gather together 2 parsnip batons and 2 orange, 2 yellow, and 2 purple carrot batons, wrap half a pancetta slice around the middle of the bundle to secure it, and place seam-side-down on the prepared sheet pan. Scatter the thyme leaves over the bundles.

Roast the bundles until the pancetta is crisp and the vegetables have colored a little, about 20 minutes. Transfer to a serving platter and serve immediately.

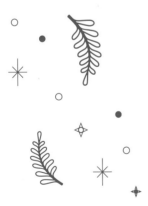

SUN-BLUSH TOMATO, PESTO, AND GOAT CHEESE STARS

These flavorful, little pastry stars can be made in a flash, and they will disappear equally fast! You can try different fillings, but this combination of tomato, pesto, and goat cheese is a perfect match for the season.

Flour for the work surface

¾ lb (340 g) store-bought puff pastry, thawed according to package instructions if frozen

3½ oz (100 g) fresh goat cheese

¼ cup (50 g) good-quality basil pesto

¼ cup (50 g) drained sun-blush (semi-dried) tomatoes in olive oil (see Chef's Note), finely diced

Small fresh sweet basil sprigs for garnish

MAKES 24 MINI PASTRIES

Have ready a 24-cup mini muffin pan. On a lightly floured work surface, unroll the sheet of pastry. Using a 2¾-inch (7-cm) star-shaped cutter, cut out 24 stars. Carefully transfer each star to a muffin cup, pressing it gently against the bottom and extending the points up the sides, to form a tartlet shell. Spoon a generous ½ teaspoon of the cheese onto the bottom of each tartlet shell. Chill for 20 minutes. While the pastry is chilling, preheat the oven to 400°F (200°C).

Bake the pastry until golden and crisp, 12–15 minutes. Remove from the oven and spoon about 1 teaspoon of the pesto into half of the pastry shells and then divide the tomato evenly among the remaining shells. Arrange on a platter, scatter the basil around the stars, and serve immediately.

✳ CHEF'S NOTE

Be sure to purchase semi-dried tomatoes in oil, known as sun-blush tomatoes in Britain, for this recipe, as oil-packed sun-dried tomatoes will be too firm.

MINI TURKEY AND CRANBERRY SAUSAGE ROLLS

Every good Christmas party needs sausage rolls on the menu, and this version, which is bursting with festive flavors, is the perfect choice.

Flour for the work surface

¾ lb (340 g) store-bought puff pastry, thawed according to package instructions if frozen

About ¾ lb (340 g) turkey or chicken chipolata sausages (10 sausages) (see Chef's Note)

¼ cup (80 g) wild cranberry sauce

1 egg, beaten, for brushing

MAKES ABOUT 40 ROLLS

Preheat the oven to 375°F (190°C).

On a lightly floured work surface, unroll the sheet of pastry. Slit the skins on the sausages, peel them off and discard, and set the sausages to one side. Starting ¼ inch (6 mm) in from a short edge of the pastry sheet, spread a line of cranberry sauce ⅜ inch (1 cm) wide along the width of the pastry. Lay 2 sausages, end to end, on top of the cranberry sauce; they should reach to the edge of the pastry on both ends; trim as needed. Roll the edge of the pastry around the sausages and seal it with a little water where it meets the pastry sheet. Then, using a sharp knife, cut along the edge of the roll to form 1 long sausage roll. Place the roll, seam side down, on a cutting board and cut crosswise into about eight 1¼-inch (3-cm) sausage rolls. Carefully transfer the rolls to a sheet pan, spacing them about 1 inch (2.5 cm) apart. Repeat four times with the remaining pastry and sausages to make about 40 sausage rolls total.

Brush the sausage rolls with the beaten egg and bake until the pastry is golden and crisp, 15–20 minutes. Transfer to a serving plate and serve warm.

✴CHEF'S NOTE

Chipolatas are long, thin fresh sausages typically made of pork and weighing about 1¼ oz (35 g) each. A great tradition in Britain, they are often part of a full breakfast, with bacon, eggs, tomatoes, and mushrooms. Wrapped in bacon and called "pigs in blankets," they are also served alongside roast turkey for Christmas dinner. They can be difficult to find in the United States, so any long, thin sausage of about the same size can be substituted.

Mini Rösti with Salmon and Chive Crème Fraîche

The rösti can be made ahead of time and reheated just before serving. Bigger ones, topped with smoked salmon, a little baby spinach, a poached egg, and hollandaise sauce, make a celebratory Christmas Day breakfast dish.

FOR THE RÖSTI

1 russet potato, about 3½ oz (100 g)

1 tablespoon cornstarch

4 teaspoons butter, melted

Fine sea salt and freshly ground black pepper

1 tablespoon roughly chopped fresh dill

FOR THE TOPPING

¼ cup (60 g) crème fraîche

1 tablespoon finely chopped fresh chives

Finely grated zest and juice of 1 lemon

5½ oz (150 g) thinly sliced smoked salmon

Freshly ground black pepper

Tiny fresh dill sprigs

MAKES 12 MINI RÖSTI

To make the rösti, peel the potato, then grate on the large holes of a box grater. Transfer the potato to a colander and press against it with a spatula to force out all the moisture. Scoop the potato into a bowl, add the cornstarch and butter, and mix well. Season with salt and pepper, then stir in the dill.

Heat a large nonstick frying pan over medium-high heat. Add a tablespoonful of the potato mixture and flatten slightly with the back of the spoon. Repeat to form more rösti, being careful not to crowd the pan. Cook, turning once, until crisp and golden on both sides, 2–3 minutes on each side. Transfer to paper towels to drain. Repeat with the remaining potato mixture. (Because butter is mixed with the potato, there is no need to add oil or butter to the pan to cook the rösti.) Let cool slightly.

To make the topping, in a small bowl, combine the crème fraîche, chives, and lemon zest and mix well.

To serve, top each rösti with a dollop of the crème fraîche mixture and a twist of smoked salmon. Drizzle a few drops of lemon juice onto the salmon and add a twist of pepper and a dill sprig or two. Serve immediately.

SKEWERS OF TOMATO, BASIL, AND MOZZARELLA

These simple skewers add a fabulous burst of seasonal color to a plate of Christmas nibbles and are very quick to assemble. If possible, use a selection of red, yellow, and orange tomatoes for a particularly eye-catching presentation.

FOR EACH SKEWER

1 bamboo skewer

1 small vine-ripened tomato, halved

1 small fresh mozzarella ball (bocconcino), halved

1 small fresh Greek basil sprig or large fresh sweet basil leaf

1 piece drained sun-blush (semi-dried) tomato in olive oil (see Chef's Note, page 111)

MAKES 1 SKEWER

Onto a small bamboo skewer, thread ½ vine-ripened tomato, ½ mozzarella ball, the basil, the sun-blush tomato, the remaining ½ mozzarella ball, and finish with the remaining ½ vine-ripened tomato.

Repeat the process to make as many skewers as you like.

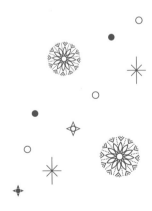

CORN TORTILLA CUPS WITH CRUSHED AVOCADO AND ASPARAGUS TIPS

For the deluxe version of these lovely vegetable-laden cups, top each one with a small piece of thin, crisp bacon and a few toasted pine nuts.

7 corn tortillas, each about 6 inches (15 cm) in diameter

Avocado oil for brushing and drizzling

1 large ripe avocado, halved, pitted, and peeled

Juice of ½ lime

½ small fresh red chile, sliced paper-thin

Fine sea salt and freshly ground black pepper

40 asparagus spear tips, cooked tender-crisp

2 tablespoons pomegranate seeds for garnish

Handful of cress for garnish

MAKES 20 MINI CUPS

Preheat the oven to 325°F (165°C). Have ready a 24-cup mini muffin pan or twenty 1¼-inch (3-cm) fluted tartlet pans.

Using a 2¾-inch (7-cm) plain round cutter, cut out 20 rounds from the tortillas. Press each round into a muffin cup or a tartlet pan and then brush with a little oil. If using the tartlet pans, place them on a large sheet pan. Bake the tortilla cups until crisp, 8–10 minutes. Let cool in the pan(s) on a wire rack to room temperature.

While the cups are cooling, in a small bowl, crush the avocado with a fork and mix in the lime juice and chile. Season to taste with salt and pepper. Cover and keep in a cool place until needed.

To assemble, spoon a little of the crushed avocado into each cup. Arrange 2 asparagus tips on top, drizzle with a little oil, and sprinkle with the pomegranate seeds and cress. Serve at once.

BLENHEIM PALACE

An Abundance of Fruits and Nuts

Named for an early eighteenth-century battle in the Spanish War of Succession, Blenheim is a country house in the small market town of Woodstock, in Oxfordshire. One of England's largest homes, the three-hundred-year-old palace is the seat of the Dukes of Marlborough and is best known as the birthplace and ancestral home of Winston Churchill.

It was Queen Anne who initially funded the foundations of Blenheim Palace, before the 1st Duke of Marlborough fell out of favor. In 1711, Mary Eales, confectioner to Queen Anne, included a recipe "to sugar all sorts of small fruit" in her book, *Mrs Mary Eales's Receipts*. This was easily achieved by coating the fruits in a mixture of egg white and sugar before drying them on the stove. Sugared fruits and nuts seasoned with spices, called comfits, were hugely popular in the 1700s and traditionally would have adorned many a table at Christmastime.

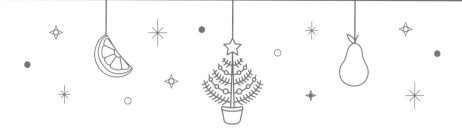

To this day, fruits and nuts in their many guises are a big part of Christmas fare and gifting. Each year, Blenheim Palace hosts a wonderful Christmas market at which street-food vendors sell a wide range of enticing traditional and contemporary treats, many of them featuring these centuries-old favorite ingredients.

From the glorious Christmas Crown Pavlova and the simple yet stunning Caramelized Walnut and Honey Tart to the indispensable seasonal mince pies, all the recipes in this chapter shine a light on the joy of cooking creatively with fruits and nuts.

White Chocolate Tiffin

This "melt-and-mix" tiffin is very quick to make. The tart cranberries and apricots contrast beautifully with the sweetness of the white chocolate, the ginger biscuits are delightfully crunchy, and the pistachios add a splash of color. For those who prefer something less sweet, it can be made with dark chocolate, and the fruits and nuts can also be varied. This tiffin makes a lovely gift presented in a box or an eco-cellophane bag tied with festive ribbon.

12 oz (340 g) white chocolate, chopped

6½ tablespoons (100 g) unsalted butter, cut into small pieces

2 tablespoons golden syrup or honey

½ cup (60 g) plump unsweetened dried cranberries

½ cup (60 g) soft dried apricots, sliced

½ cup (60 g) pistachios, coarsely chopped

3½ oz (100 g) ginger biscuits, crushed

MAKES 16 SMALL SQUARES

Line the bottom and sides of an 8-inch (20-cm) square baking pan with parchment paper, extending the parchment above the rim to use for lifting the tiffin out of the pan.

Put 9 oz (250 g) of the chocolate and the butter into a heatproof bowl placed over (not touching) simmering water in a saucepan and heat, stirring often, until melted and smooth. Alternatively, heat in a microwave using 20-second bursts and stirring after each burst. White chocolate burns very easily, so use low heat on the stove top or medium power in the microwave and stir often. Lastly, mix in the golden syrup.

Set aside a couple of small handfuls of the cranberries, apricots, and nuts for sprinkling on top. Add the remaining fruits and nuts and the biscuits to the chocolate mixture and mix well. Transfer to the prepared pan and press into the bottom in an even layer. Let cool, then cover and chill for 1 hour.

Melt the remaining 3 oz (90 g) chocolate. Using a palette knife or an offset spatula, spread half of the chocolate in an even layer over the top of the tiffin. Sprinkle the reserved fruits and nuts evenly over the chocolate, then drizzle the remaining melted chocolate over the top. Let set for 20 minutes, then lift out the tiffin and cut into small squares.

The tiffin squares will keep in an airtight container in the refrigerator for up to 2 weeks.

ICED CHRISTMAS PUDDING

Many people find traditional Christmas pudding very heavy, particularly after eating roast turkey and all the trimmings. This is a brilliant alternative. Like the classic, it is made with lots of dried fruit and some alcohol, but it is delightfully refreshing. Served alongside little Mince Pies (page 128), it is the perfect end to a special Christmas dinner.

3 tablespoons diced candied orange peel

¼ cup (30 g) plump unsweetened dried cranberries

6 tablespoons (50 g) soft dried apricots, diced

½ cup (50 g) plump dried cherries

½ cup (50 g) soft dried figs, finely chopped

3½ tablespoons (50 ml) Madeira, sherry, or cherry brandy

⅔ cup (30 g) mini marshmallows

3 tablespoons small chocolate chips

1⅔ cups (400 ml) vanilla ice cream, slightly soft

⅓ cup plus 2 tablespoons (100 g) plain Greek yogurt

2 tablespoons maple syrup

1 teaspoon pure vanilla extract

Fresh fruits, edible flowers, and/or herb sprigs of choice for garnish

MAKES 6–8 SERVINGS

Line a 2½-cup (600-ml) pudding basin with plastic wrap and place in the freezer.

In a small bowl, combine the candied peel, cranberries, apricots, cherries, and figs. Pour the Madeira over the fruit, toss, cover, and leave to macerate at room temperature for several hours or up to overnight.

Line the bottom and sides of a small sheet pan with plastic wrap. Tip the fruit onto the prepared pan, spread it out in an even layer, and freeze for 30 minutes. Put the marshmallows and chocolate chips into a small bowl and place in the freezer at the same time.

In a bowl, combine the ice cream, yogurt, maple syrup, and vanilla. Using a wooden spoon or rubber spatula, and working quickly so the ice cream does not melt too much, mix together well. Stir in the fruit, chocolate, and marshmallows from the freezer, distributing them evenly. Spoon into the chilled pudding basin, packing it down well with the back of a spoon. Cover with plastic wrap and return to the freezer. Freeze for at least 4 hours or up to overnight before serving.

To serve, remove the basin from the freezer. Dip the bottom 2 inches (5 cm) of the basin in warm water for 30 seconds, then invert a serving plate on top of the basin, invert the basin and plate together, lift off the basin, and peel off the plastic wrap. Garnish with fresh fruits, such as figs or cherries; flowers; and/or herb sprigs, such as thyme or rosemary.

✳ CHEF'S NOTE

This pudding is delicious served with warm chocolate sauce and brandy snaps (page 96) or fresh cherries.

Packing the pudding into small pudding basins ideal for one serving can be less wasteful than using a large basin, as once the pudding melts, it does not refreeze well.

MINCE PIES

According to custom, for each mince pie you eat between Christmas and Twelfth Night, you will have a happy month in the new year, making these little mince pies an essential part of Christmas preparations. Be sure that you have enough for everyone to have at least twelve, thus ensuring happiness all year long! The light, crunchy macaroon topping on half of the pies is a delectable addition and can be made with either almonds or coconut.

FOR THE PASTRY

1¾ cups plus 2 tablespoons (225 g) flour, plus more for the work surface

¼ cup (50 g) superfine sugar

⅔ cup (140 g) butter, at room temperature

1 egg yolk lightly beaten with 1 tablespoon cold water

Optional flavorings: 1 teaspoon finely grated orange zest, ½ teaspoon mixed spice (see Chef's Note, page 21), or ½ teaspoon pure almond or vanilla extract

FOR THE FILLING

¾ cup plus 1 tablespoon (250 g) Christmas Mincemeat (page 144)

To make the pastry, in a food processor, combine the flour, superfine sugar, and butter and process until the mixture is the texture of fine bread crumbs. Add the egg yolk–water mixture and a flavoring, if desired, and pulse a few times to mix. Tip into a bowl and bring together by hand to form a smooth dough.

Preheat the oven to 350°F (180°C). Have ready mini muffin pans to make 30 pies or thirty 1½-inch (4-cm) tartlet molds.

On a lightly floured work surface, roll out the dough no more than ¼ inch (6 mm) thick. Using a 2½-inch (6-cm) plain round cutter, cut out 30 rounds. Transfer the rounds to the muffin cups or tartlet molds, pressing them gently against the bottom and up the sides. Then, using a 1½-inch (4-cm) star-shaped cutter, cut out 15 stars, gathering up the scraps, pressing them together, and rerolling the dough as needed to yield enough stars. Keep the stars on one side. If using tartlet molds, transfer them to a large sheet pan.

To fill, place a teaspoonful of the mincemeat in each pastry-lined mold. Chill the filled pastry for 10 minutes.

Recipe continues on the following page

continued from the previous page

FOR THE MACAROON TOPPING

1 egg white

¼ cup (50 g) superfine sugar

⅔ cup (60 g) ground almonds or unsweetened shredded dried coconut

3½ tablespoons sliced almonds or unsweetened dried coconut flakes for decorating

Tiny white, silver, and/or gold sugar balls and/or pearl sugar (see Chef's Note, page 16) for decorating the star-topped pies (optional)

Confectioners' sugar for dusting

Makes thirty 1½-inch (4-cm) pies

While the pastry is chilling, make the macaroon topping. To make an almond macaroon topping, in a small bowl, whisk the egg white until foamy and thick, then whisk in the superfine sugar until stiff peaks form. Fold in the ground almonds just until evenly mixed. To make a coconut macaroon topping, substitute the coconut for the almonds.

Spoon the topping neatly onto half of the mince pies (or pipe it on using a piping bag fitted with a small plain tip). For the almond macaroon topping, decorate with the sliced almonds. For the coconut macaroon topping, sprinkle with the coconut flakes. Place the pastry stars on the top of the remaining mince pies and decorate with tiny sugar balls or pearl sugar, if using.

Bake the pies until the pastry is crisp and golden, 12–15 minutes. The macaroon topping browns quickly, so keep a close eye on it. Let cool in the muffin cups or tartlet molds on wire racks for 5 minutes, then ease the pies out of the pans and let cool on the racks.

These pies are most delicious when served warm. Lightly dust them with confectioners' sugar just before serving.

The pies will keep in an airtight container at room temperature for up to 2 weeks. They can be warmed in a 325°F (165°C) oven for 5 minutes before serving.

CROWN PAVLOVA

*This pavlova makes a noble centerpiece for Christmas dinner. The white meringue
with its tiny silver sparkles and filling of red fruits and fresh green herb sprigs looks
fantastically festive. However, a "tropical" crown filled with mango, passion fruit,
pomegranate, pineapple, kiwifruit, and star fruit and sprinkled with toasted coconut
flakes is equally spectacular.*

FOR THE MERINGUE

1½ cups (300 g) superfine sugar

⅔ cup (160 g) egg whites (from about 5 eggs)

Vegetable oil for the tart ring

Pearl sugar (see Chef's Note, page 16) and tiny silver sugar balls for decorating

FOR THE FILLING

⅔ cup (150 ml) heavy cream

⅓ cup plus 1½ tablespoons (100 g) crème fraîche

2 tablespoons superfine sugar

1 teaspoon pure vanilla extract

7 oz (200 g) cherries and mixed fresh berries, such as strawberries, raspberries, and blueberries

2 small fresh figs, stemmed and quartered lengthwise

1 nectarine, halved, pitted, and cut into 8 slices

2 tablespoons pomegranate seeds

Few fresh rosemary and/or mint sprigs

Few small edible flowers

MAKES 8 SERVINGS

To make the meringue, position 2 oven racks in the center of the oven and preheat the oven to 400°F (200°C). Line 2 large sheet pans with parchment paper or silicone baking mats.

Spread the superfine sugar in a thin, even layer on a prepared sheet pan and place it in the oven for 5 minutes. Meanwhile, in a stand mixer fitted with the whip attachment, beat the egg whites on medium-high speed until stiff peaks form.

Remove the superfine sugar from the oven and reduce the oven temperature to 250°F (120°C). With the mixer running at high speed, add the sugar a spoonful at a time, beating after each addition until the meringue comes back up to stiff peaks. Once all the sugar has been added, continue to beat for a further 3–5 minutes. The meringue is ready to use if it forms smooth, shiny peaks when the whip attachment is lifted out of it.

Rub oil around the inside of an 8-inch (20-cm) metal tart ring. Place it on a prepared sheet pan. Spoon half of the meringue into the tart ring, using a palette knife or offset spatula to spread it to the edges and to smooth the top. It will be about 2 inches (5 cm) deep. Sprinkle with a little pearl sugar. Carefully lift off the ring. It should slip off easily, leaving a neat edge.

Recipe continues on the following page

continued from the previous page

Wash the ring, dry it well, and rub oil around the inside again. Place it on the second prepared sheet pan. Spoon the remaining meringue into a piping bag fitted with a ⅜-inch (1-cm) star tip. Pipe large rosettes around the entire inside edge of the ring. Pipe a second row on top of the first row, and then pipe a third row, leaving gaps between the rosettes on the top row. Carefully slip off the tart ring as before. Sprinkle the meringue ring with the pearl sugar and silver balls.

Bake both meringues, switching the pans between the racks and rotating them back to front at the halfway point, until they are completely dry, 45–60 minutes. They should remain bright white during baking without the slightest hint of color. Let cool completely on the pans on wire racks. Once cool, remove them very carefully, as they can break easily. The meringues can be stored in large airtight containers at room temperature until ready to use. They will keep for up to 1 week.

To fill the pavlova, place the meringue base on a serving plate. In the stand mixer fitted with the whisk attachment on medium-high speed or in a bowl with a balloon whisk, beat together the cream, crème fraîche, superfine sugar, and vanilla until medium peaks form. Be careful not to overwhip. Spoon one-fourth of the cream into a piping bag fitted with the ⅜-inch (1-cm) star tip and pipe a line of cream all around the circumference of the meringue base. Very carefully position the piped meringue ring on the base; the cream will secure it in place.

Spoon the remaining cream into the center of the pavlova and spread it to the edges with a palette knife or offset spatula. Arrange the cherries and berries, figs, nectarines, and pomegranate seeds on top of the cream and arrange the herb sprigs and flowers among the fruits. Serve within 1 hour.

Tipsy Tart with Mixed Fruits

Tipsy tart, also known as Cape brandy tart, is a traditional South African dessert and, despite the name, is a pudding, not a tart. Like the popular sticky toffee pudding, it is made with dates, but it is lighter and is drenched in brandy syrup rather than rich butterscotch sauce. Topped with a garnish of mixed fruits, it makes a delicious alternative to Christmas pudding. Serve with whipped cream or alongside the Iced Christmas Pudding on page 127.

3½ tablespoons butter, at room temperature, plus more for the pie dish

7 oz (200 g) pitted dates, chopped

¾ cup plus 2 tablespoons (200 ml) boiling water

1 teaspoon baking soda

¾ cup plus 1½ tablespoons (180 g) firmly packed dark brown sugar

2 eggs

1 cup plus 3 tablespoons (150 g) flour

1 teaspoon baking powder

Pinch of salt

⅓ cup plus 1½ tablespoons (40 g) pecans, chopped

FOR THE BRANDY SYRUP

1 cup (200 g) granulated sugar

¾ cup (180 ml) water

⅓ cup plus 1½ tablespoons (100 ml) brandy

1 tablespoon butter

1 teaspoon pure vanilla extract

FOR THE DECORATION

Mixed fruits, such as 1 blood orange, 2 small figs, 2 apricots, and 4 Cape gooseberries

Few small fresh mint or rosemary sprigs

MAKES 8 SERVINGS

Preheat the oven to 350°F (180°C). Butter a 9-inch (23-cm) round pie dish.

In a bowl, combine the dates, boiling water, and baking soda and let stand for 10 minutes. Meanwhile, in a second bowl, beat together the butter and sugar until light and creamy. Add the eggs and beat until well mixed. Sift together the flour, baking powder, and salt, and fold into the butter mixture until incorporated. Then stir in the pecans and the dates and their water, mixing well. Transfer the batter to the prepared pie dish.

Bake the tart for 40–45 minutes. It will be quite dark when ready and should feel spongy when lightly pressed with a fingertip. Transfer to a wire rack and prick several times with a fork.

About 15 minutes before the tart is ready, begin making the brandy syrup. In a heavy saucepan, combine the granulated sugar and water and bring to a boil over medium-high heat, stirring to dissolve the sugar. Adjust the heat to a simmer and simmer until the mixture is syrupy, about 5 minutes. Add the brandy, butter, and vanilla, return to a boil, and then remove from the heat. Pour the hot syrup over the hot tart and let stand until all the syrup soaks in.

The tart can be served warm or at room temperature. Just before serving, peel, pit, and cut, section, or slice the fruits as needed and arrange decoratively on the tart along with the herb sprigs.

CARAMELIZED WALNUT AND HONEY TART

The simple appearance of this tart belies how wonderful it tastes. Whether you serve it with a scoop of vanilla ice cream at the end of a meal, as part of a festive afternoon tea, or simply with a cup of coffee, one slice is never enough! It echoes the traditional Swiss regional favorite Engadiner Nusstorte.

FOR THE PASTRY

2⅓ cups (300 g) flour, plus more for the work surface

¾ cup (150 g) superfine sugar

¾ cup plus 2 tablespoons (200 g) cold butter, diced

1 egg, lightly beaten

Pinch of salt

FOR THE FILLING

1¼ cups (250 g) granulated sugar

2⅔ cups (300 g) walnut pieces, coarsely chopped

¾ cup plus 2 tablespoons (200 ml) heavy cream, heated

1 tablespoon honey

1 teaspoon pure vanilla extract

Confectioners' sugar for dusting

MAKES 6–8 SERVINGS

To make the pastry, in a food processor, combine the flour, superfine sugar, and butter and pulse until the mixture is the texture of coarse bread crumbs. Add the egg and salt, pulse a few more times, and then tip into a bowl and bring together by hand to form a smooth dough. Divide the dough in half, wrap each half in plastic wrap, and chill for 20 minutes.

To make the filling, put the granulated sugar into a nonstick frying pan and heat gently over low heat until it starts to caramelize. Toss the walnuts into the pan and continue to cook over low heat for a couple of minutes, shaking the pan often to ensure all the nuts are coated in the caramel. Remove from the heat and pour in the warm cream, honey, and vanilla. Stir well and return the pan to low heat for a minute or two to blend the cream with the walnuts. Set aside to cool.

Preheat the oven to 325°F (165°C). Have ready an 8¾-inch (22-cm) flan ring with 1½-inch (4-cm) fluted sides. Place the ring on the center of a sheet pan.

Recipe continues on the following page

continued from the previous page

On a lightly floured work surface, roll out half of the pastry into a round ¼ inch (6 mm) thick and at least 12 inches (30 cm) in diameter for the shell. Line the flan ring with the pastry round, easing it gently into the ring, fitting it snugly along the bottom rim, pressing it firmly onto the sides, and then trimming it neatly along the top rim. Place in the refrigerator to chill. Gather up the dough scraps, press together, and set aside. Roll out the other half the same way for the lid and decorations. First cut out an 8¾-inch (22-cm) round to cover the top of the tart. Then, using a small holly leaf–shaped cutter (or another shape of your choice), cut out about 15 leaves, rerolling the dough scraps as needed to yield enough leaves. To make holly berries, roll 5 small pieces of dough into 5 balls.

Remove the tart base from the refrigerator and fill with the nut mixture, spreading it to the edges. Lay the pastry round over the tart and press down around the edges to seal. Arrange the leaves on the top in an attractive pattern, sticking each one down by brushing it with a little water, and then add the berries the same way.

Bake the tart until the pastry is golden and crisp, 50–60 minutes. If the tart is browning too much, cover it loosely with a sheet of parchment paper or aluminum foil. Let cool on the pan on a wire rack for 10 minutes, then carefully lift off the flan ring.

Carefully transfer the tart to a serving plate and serve warm or at room temperature. Dust the top with confectioners' sugar just before serving. The tart will keep in an airtight container at room temperature for up to 1 week.

Caernarfon Castle

Preserves and Savory Condiments

Caernarfon Castle, a noble example of medieval architecture located on the banks of the Seiont River in Gwynedd, northwest Wales, was built long before the time when Christmas was celebrated around a table laden with beautiful fresh food. The only way to keep food for any length of time in those days was to salt it, dry it, or pickle it. Dried meat and fish, salted butters, and relishes were all popular methods of preserving food that were used when Edward I, who ordered the building of Caernarfon Castle, resided within its walls in the late thirteenth century.

The season of Advent, in the run up to Christmas, was all about fasting, but when the nobility and the wealthy did eat, they would have enjoyed some rich fare, including boar, beef, venison, cheeses, and wine. What better way to accompany all of these foods than with plenty of preserves? The early medieval period was also the time of the Crusades, when dried fruits and spices were being introduced into England from the Middle East and the practice of mixing shredded meat with spices and sweet ingredients developed. This "mincemeat" would be enclosed in hard pastry as a means of

containing it as it cooked. Only later did the pastry become an edible component of the pie. By the seventeenth century, mince pies were established as a Christmas tradition. Thankfully, today you won't find shredded meat in your mince pie!

This chapter showcases some spectacular preserves and tracklements (savory condiments) to bring a patch of color and burst of flavor to any Christmas feast.

CHRISTMAS MINCEMEAT

This mincemeat is so much nicer than any of the commercially made ones, and it is very easy to make. Traditionally, it contains shredded suet (raw, hard fat from beef or lamb), but I have used coconut oil instead, which is healthier, vegan, and imparts a lovely flavor. When the mincemeat is in the oven, it fills the house with a very evocative Christmassy aroma! The Bramley, the best-known cooking apple in Britain, is used here, but any good, tart cooking apple will work.

18 oz (500 g) Bramley apples, peeled, cored, and finely diced

1¼ cups (180 g) mixed dark and golden raisins and dried currants

1½ cups (180 g) plump unsweetened dried cranberries

⅔ cup (100 g) soft dried figs, diced

6 tablespoons (50 g) soft dried apricots, diced

Finely grated zest and juice of 2 oranges

Finely grated zest and juice of 1 lemon

¾ cup (150 g) firmly packed dark muscovado sugar

1 teaspoon mixed spice (see Chef's Note, page 21)

1 teaspoon ground cinnamon

½ teaspoon freshly grated nutmeg

⅓ cup plus 2 tablespoons (100 g) coconut oil

3½ tablespoons (50 ml) brandy or sherry

MAKES THREE ¾-PINT (350-ML) JARS

In a large bowl, combine the apples, raisins and currants, cranberries, figs, apricots, citrus zests and juices, sugar, mixed spice, cinnamon, nutmeg, and coconut oil and mix thoroughly. Cover the bowl with a clean kitchen towel and leave in a cool place overnight or for up to 12 hours to allow the flavors to develop.

Preheat the oven to 250°F (120°C). Transfer the mixture to a roasting pan or large, shallow baking dish and cover loosely with aluminum foil. Bake for 3–4 hours, removing the pan every 30 minutes to give the mixture a good stir. The mincemeat is done when the apple is soft, dark, and has broken down.

Remove from the oven and stir in the brandy. Pack into 3 sterilized ¾-pint (350-ml) canning jars (see Chef's Note) and let cool completely. Cover with a waxed sealing disc and cap tightly. The jars can be stored in a cool, dark place for up to 1 year. Refrigerate after opening.

✳ CHEF'S NOTE

Here is an easy method for sterilizing glass jars and bottles: Wash jars or bottles and lids in hot, soapy water, rinse well with kettle-boiled water, and dry with a clean kitchen towel or paper towel. Set the jars upside down on a wire rack over a sheet pan and place in an oven preheated to 350°F (180°C) until completely dry, about 5 minutes. Fill the jars or bottles while they are still warm from the oven. To sterilize two-part canning lids—screw band and flat lid with a rubber ring on the underside—immerse them in simmering (not boiling) water for about 10 minutes, then drain and dry well with a kitchen towel or paper towel.

Fill the jars or bottles as directed, then wipe the rims clean, cap tightly, and let cool completely. Check for a good seal after 24 hours by pressing on the center of the lid. If it remains depressed, the seal is good. Refrigerate any jar that fails the test.

You can substitute other dried fruits for the ones listed here, keeping the quantities the same.

As the mincemeat cools, the coconut oil may separate a little and solidify in small blobs. This is normal, and it will blend in again when the mincemeat is used in baking.

Passion Fruit Curd

Quick to make and very versatile, this flavorful curd is definitely worth having on hand at Christmastime. Use it as an unctuous cake filling, spread it on toast or scones, pipe it into brandy snaps (page 96), use it as a tartlet or profiterole filling, add a dollop to a bowl of Greek yogurt or vanilla ice cream, or fold it into crème fraîche and serve with fresh berries and baby meringues for a delectable dessert.

8–10 large passion fruits

1 cup (200 g) superfine sugar

⅔ cup (140 g) butter

Finely grated zest of 1 large orange

2 eggs, lightly beaten

MAKES ONE 1-PINT
(475-ML) JAR

Place a fine-mesh sieve over a bowl. Halve the passion fruits, scoop the pulp into the sieve, and press against the pulp and seeds with the back of a spoon to force out all the juice. Measure out ½ cup (120 ml) juice.

Pour water to a depth of about 2 inches (5 cm) into the bottom pan of a double boiler. In the top pan, combine the passion fruit juice, sugar, butter, and orange zest and place on top of the bottom pan, making sure the top pan is not touching the water. Set over medium heat and stir until the butter melts and the sugar is fully dissolved. Then whisk in the eggs and cook, stirring constantly, until the curd has thickened and coats the back of a spoon, 10–15 minutes.

Remove from the heat and transfer to a sterilized 1-pint (475-ml) jar (see Chef's Note, page 145). Let cool, then cap tightly. The curd will keep in the refrigerator for up to 1 month.

✳ CHEF'S NOTE

You can substitute ½ cup (120 ml) fresh lemon juice, blood orange juice, lime juice, or grapefruit juice for the passion fruit juice.

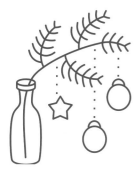

SPICED ORANGE SLICES

This recipe came from my mother, who always made these orange slices for Christmas using homegrown fruit. We lived in South Africa, where Christmas Day was hot, so instead of the traditional roast turkey and ham, roast potatoes, and Brussels sprouts, we had cold turkey and ham with lots of wonderful salads and homemade tracklements, including chutney, cherry guava jelly, pickled (homegrown) walnuts, pickled red cabbage, and piccalilli (mustard pickled vegetables). It was really a meal of Mum's fabulous preserves, with a little turkey and salad on the side!

5 large oranges

1¼ cups (300 ml) cider vinegar

2¼ cups (450 g) sugar

8 whole cloves

8 juniper berries

2 cinnamon sticks, each 2 inches (5 cm) long

MAKES TWO 1-PINT (475-ML) JARS

Cut the oranges crosswise into slices ⅜ inch (1 cm) thick, discarding the end slices and removing the seeds. Put the slices into a saucepan, add water to cover, and bring to a boil over high heat. Reduce the heat to a simmer, cover, and simmer gently until the peel is soft enough to squeeze between your fingers, about 15 minutes. Using a slotted spoon, carefully lift out the orange slices and place them in a large bowl. Discard the water.

Put the vinegar, sugar, cloves, juniper berries, and cinnamon into the saucepan and stir together over low heat to dissolve the sugar. Raise the heat to medium-high, bring to a boil, and add the orange slices. Adjust the heat to a simmer and simmer gently, uncovered, until the orange slices are glazed with the syrup, about 30 minutes.

Using the slotted spoon, carefully transfer the orange slices and spices to 2 sterilized 1-pint (475-ml) canning jars (see Chef's Note, page 145), dividing them evenly between the jars. Return the pan to medium-high heat, bring the syrup to a boil, and boil until reduced by half, 10–15 minutes.

Ladle the syrup over the orange slices, covering them completely and leaving ½-inch (12-mm) headspace. Carefully slide a thin-bladed knife down the inside edge of each jar and move it all along the edge to pop any air bubbles trapped between the orange slices, then cap tightly. The orange slices will keep in a cool, dark place for up to 2 years. Refrigerate after opening.

Tomato and Sweet Red Pepper Relish

Serve this richly seasoned relish with cold meats, with cheese, on a ploughman's platter, or with frittata. To make the ultimate cheese toastie (aka grilled cheese sandwich), use sourdough bread with farmhouse butter, sharp Cheddar cheese, and lashings of this relish.

3¼ lb (1.5 kg) ripe tomatoes, peeled and coarsely chopped

14 oz (400 g) yellow onions, thinly sliced

3 large red bell peppers, seeded and diced

2 cloves garlic, crushed

1½ cups (350 ml) red wine vinegar

1½ tablespoons yellow mustard seeds

1 tablespoon medium curry powder

½ teaspoon cayenne pepper

1½ cups (300 g) sugar

2 teaspoons sea salt

Makes four 10-fl oz (300-ml) jars

In a large, heavy saucepan, combine the tomatoes, onions, peppers, garlic, vinegar, mustard seeds, curry powder, and cayenne, stir well, and bring to a boil over medium-high heat, stirring occasionally. Reduce the heat to a simmer and simmer uncovered, stirring occasionally, until the mixture is pulpy, about 40 minutes.

Add the sugar and salt, reduce the heat to low, and stir until the sugar dissolves. Raise the heat to medium-high, return to a boil, and cook uncovered at a gentle boil, stirring often, until much of the liquid has been absorbed and the relish is thick, 30–40 minutes.

Transfer to 4 sterilized 10-fl oz (300-ml) canning jars (see Chef's Note, page 145), leaving ½-inch (12-mm) headspace, and cap tightly. The relish will keep in a cool, dark place for up to 1 year. Refrigerate after opening.

SPICY PEAR CHUTNEY

This chutney is the perfect accompaniment to cold ham and turkey, and pairs particularly well with Swiss cheese. Leave it in the jar for 1 month before using to allow the flavors to develop.

2 lb (1 kg) pears, peeled, cored, and diced

7 oz (200 g) yellow onions, thinly sliced

3½ oz (100 g) pitted dates (12–13 dates), finely chopped

Finely grated zest and juice of 1 orange

1 clove garlic, crushed

¾-inch (2-cm) piece fresh ginger, peeled and grated

1 teaspoon yellow mustard seeds, toasted

1 teaspoon ground coriander

1 teaspoon ground cinnamon

½ teaspoon cayenne pepper

2 cups (475 ml) cider vinegar

2¼ cups (450 g) firmly packed light muscovado sugar

2 teaspoons sea salt

MAKES TWO 1-PINT (475-ML) JARS

In a large saucepan, combine the pears, onions, dates, orange zest and juice, garlic, ginger, mustard seeds, coriander, cinnamon, cayenne, and vinegar, stir well, and bring to a boil over medium-high heat, stirring occasionally. Reduce the heat to a simmer and simmer uncovered, stirring occasionally, until the mixture is pulpy, about 20 minutes.

Add the sugar and salt, reduce the heat to low, and stir until the sugar dissolves. Raise the heat to medium-high, return to a boil, and cook uncovered at a gentle boil, stirring often, until much of the liquid has been absorbed and the chutney is thick, 30–40 minutes.

Transfer to 2 sterilized 1-pint (475-ml) canning jars (see Chef's Note, page 145), leaving ½-inch (12-mm) headspace, and cap tightly. The chutney will keep in a cool, dark place for up to 1 year. Refrigerate after opening.

> ✳ CHEF'S NOTE
>
> The same amount of dried apricots or golden raisins can be used in place of the dates.

APPLE AND RED CURRANT JELLY

This glistening red jelly is a great complement to roast goose, as its acidity cuts through the richness of the meat. It is excellent with hot or cold turkey and sausages, and a generous spoonful will brighten a batch of gravy or caramelized onions. It also makes a beautiful glaze for open-face berry tarts, adding both gloss and flavor.

3¼ lb (1.5 kg) cooking apples

2 lb (1 kg) fresh or frozen red currants

4¼ cups (1 l) water

Sugar as needed (2¼ cups/450 g for every 2½ cups/600 ml juice)

MAKES FIVE 3½-FL OZ (100-ML) JARS

Roughly chop the apples (no need to peel or core them) and put them into a preserving pan or large, heavy saucepan. Add the red currants and water and bring to a boil over medium-high heat. Adjust the heat to a simmer and simmer uncovered, stirring occasionally, for 45 minutes.

Transfer the contents of the pan to a jelly bag and suspend the bag over a bowl. Leave to drip at room temperature overnight.

Measure the juice and return it to the pan. For every 2½ cups (600 ml) juice, add 2¼ cups (450 g) sugar to the pan, calculating a partial portion of sugar as needed to use up all the juice. Heat gently over low heat, stirring to dissolve the sugar. When all the sugar has dissolved, raise the heat to high, bring to a boil, and boil rapidly until the setting point is reached. Begin testing after 10 minutes. Remove the jelly from the heat, put a small spoonful of the boiling jelly on a saucer, and put the saucer into the freezer for a few minutes. Remove from the freezer, push the blob with a fingertip, and if it wrinkles and mounds, the jelly has reached the setting point. If not, boil for a few minutes longer and test again, always removing the jelly from the heat as you test.

Skim off any impurities from the surface of the jelly, then transfer to 5 sterilized 3½-fl oz (100-ml) canning jars (see Chef's Note, page 145), leaving ½-inch (12-mm) headspace, and cap tightly. The jelly will keep in a cool, dark place for up to 1 year. Refrigerate after opening.

✳ CHEF'S NOTE

Red currants and apples are rich in natural pectin and acid, making them perfect for making jelly without added pectin.

For spiced red currant jelly, add 6 whole cloves and a 2-inch (5-cm) cinnamon stick when boiling the fruit with the water and add 1 tablespoon red wine vinegar for each 2½ cups (600 ml) of juice.

For an herbed red currant jelly, add 3 fresh thyme or rosemary sprigs when boiling the fruit and add 1 tablespoon cider vinegar for each 2½ cups (600 ml) of juice.

Index

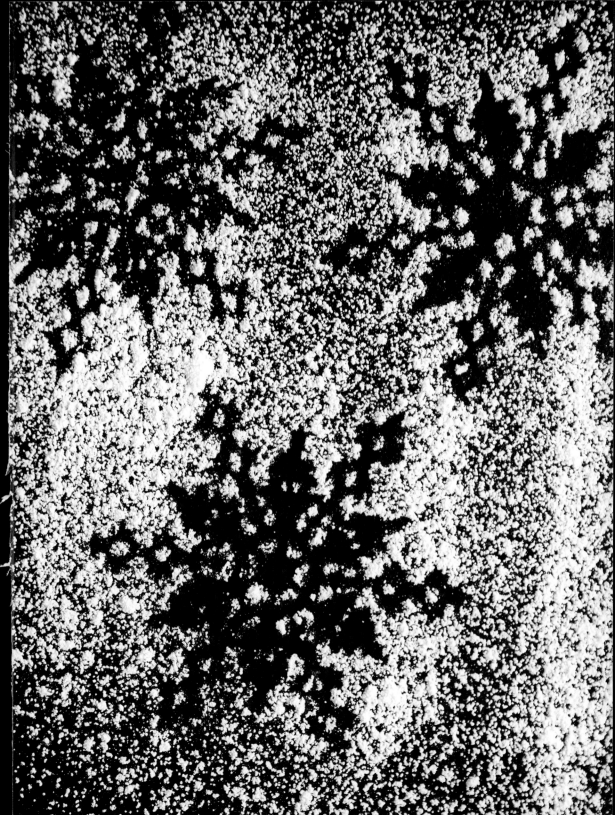

weldon**owen**

An imprint of Insight Editions
P.O. Box 3088
San Rafael, CA 94912
www.weldonowen.com

CEO Raoul Goff
VP Publisher Roger Shaw
Associate Publisher Amy Marr
Editorial Director Katie Killebrew
Assistant Editor Jourdan Plautz
VP Creative Chrissy Kwasnik
Designer Megan Sinead Harris
Production Manager Joshua Smith
Sr Production Manager,
Subsidiary Rights Lina s Palma-Temena

Photographer John Kernick

Food Stylist Carolyn Robb
Assistant Food Stylist Deirdre Reford
Prop Stylist Stephanie Bateman Sweet

Weldon Owen would also like to thank Rachel Markowitz, Sharon Silva,
and Elizabeth Parson.

Printed in China by Insight Editions
10 9 8 7 6 5 4 3 2 1

ISBN: 978-1-68188-921-4

ACKNOWLEDGMENTS

A big thank you to food historian and
author Emma Kay for her fascinating
historical contributions. John Kernick—it
was a joy working with you again on the
photographs, and thank you to Stephanie
Bateman Sweet for all your hard work
sourcing props. Deirdre Reford—your
help and creative input during the photo
shoot were brilliant, thank you so much.
I am so grateful to the team at Weldon
Owen, in particular Roger Shaw for your
ongoing support and Amy Marr for your
incredible attention to detail. Thank you
to Bill Schwartz for your introduction to
Weldon Owen.

 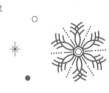

REPLANTED PAPER   ROOTS of PEACE

Insight Editions, in association with Roots of Peace, will plant two trees for each
tree used in the manufacturing of this book. Roots of Peace is an internationally
renowned humanitarian organization dedicated to eradicating land mines worldwide
and converting war-torn lands into productive farms and wildlife habitats. Roots of
Peace will plant two million fruit and nut trees in Afghanistan and provide farmers
there with the skills and support necessary for sustainable land use.